HAPPINESS

D1353721

HAPPINESS

HOW TO FIND IT AND KEEP IT

JOAN DUNCAN OLIVER

DUNCAN BAIRD PUBLISHERS

LONDON

Happiness
Joan Duncan Oliver

First published in the United Kingdom
and Ireland in 2005 by
Duncan Baird Publishers Ltd
Sixth Floor
Castle House
75–76 Wells Street
London W1T 3QH

Conceived, created and designed by
Duncan Baird Publishers

Managing Editor: Rebecca Miles
Editorial Assistant: Zoë Fargher
Managing Designer: Dan Sturges
Designer: Adelle Morris
Commissioned illustrations: Jen Cogliantry at 3+Co.

British Library Cataloguing-in-Publication Data:
A CIP record for this book is available from the
British Library

ISBN-10: 1-84483-078-0
ISBN-13: 9-781844-830787

10 9 8 7 6 5 4 3 2 1

Typeset in Frutiger and MrsEaves
Color reproduction by Colourscan, Singapore
Printed in Thailand by Imago

The abbreviations BCE and CE are used throughout
this book. BCE means Before the Common Era
(equivalent to BC); CE means of the Common Era
(equivalent to AD).

Contents

Introduction   6

Emotions
THE WAY WE FEEL
How positive feelings can change your life 14

Kindness
A CARING HEART
How to cultivate compassion   22

Uncertainty
BEFRIENDING THE UNKNOWN
**How to be content with unpredictable
outcomes**   30

Creativity
EXPRESSING YOURSELF
How to court the artist within   38

Purpose
WHAT DOES MY LIFE SERVE?
How to do what matters   48

Other People
MAKING CONNECTIONS
How to nurture friends and family   56

Time
THE CAVE AND THE POCKET
**How to balance past, present,
and future**   64

Acceptance
THE WISDOM OF LIMITS
How to be happy with what is   70

Values
LIVING YOUR TRUTH
How to find your moral compass   76

Wealth
TRUE RICHES
How much is enough?   84

Beauty
THE PLEASURE CONNECTION
How to stir the senses   92

Love
MAKING IT LAST
How to have a happy relationship   102

Laughter
THE POWER OF HUMOR
How to lighten up and live   110

Success
HAVING IT YOUR WAY
How to be a happy achiever   118

Faith
DRAWING ON THE SOURCE
How to tap sacred strength   126

Serenity
KEEPING THE PEACE
How to find your still, calm center   134

Health
WHOLE-PERSON HEALING
How happiness affects wellness
and vice versa   140

Nature
NATURAL WONDER
How Earth's infinite mysteries delight   148

Memory
VITAL RECALL
How to create happy memories,
starting now   156

Choice
FAVORABLE OPTIONS
How to make wise decisions   164

Further reading   172
Acknowledgments   173
Index   176

Introduction

A dance bandleader who died recently at the age of 97 liked to tell people he was in "the happiness business." Aren't we all, in a sense? Everyone wants to be happy, as the Dalai Lama often points out. In our fractious world, this may be the one point on which we all agree. But when it comes to the question *What is happiness?* there are probably six billion different answers— one for each person on the globe. If we're observant, we may *know* when other people are happy: the "Duchenne smile," produced by involuntary muscle contractions around the eyes and mouth, is a universal, if subtle giveaway as recognizable to a Papua New Guinean tribesman as to a British parliamentarian. What we generally *can't* tell is *why* someone's happy. Half the time, we can't even say why for ourselves. The right to pursue happiness is a wonderful opportunity, but it doesn't automatically move us closer to an answer. That may be the work of a lifetime.

Indeed, for thousands of years philosophers have argued that finding happiness is the purpose of life. The Greeks thought it was our highest moral duty. The Utilitarians, centuries later, said it was our duty to make sure everybody else was happy too. Spiritual leaders have been of mixed mind about happiness: the Christian church never has quite resolved whether it's strictly a reward of the next life or a virtue in the here and now. To the Buddhists happiness is the fruit of awakening—freedom from the agony of desire. By the time Sigmund Freud came along and psychology became our de facto religion, happiness seemed like a loaded gun. Whatever made us happy probably wasn't good for us; the pursuit of happiness was fraught with inner conflict.

Now, at long last, positive emotions like joy, affection, awe, and humor are in the spotlight. It's not just okay to seek happiness, it's essential. Our best hope of having a good life—and a safe planet—is to develop the kindlier, friendlier, more optimistic side of our nature.

A green light to pursue happiness is terrific, but where to begin? Do we look to our surroundings—work, family, our social sphere? Or do we look within, at the desires and personality traits that predispose us to be happy, and the genetic or behavioral quirks that prevent us from feeling unalloyed joy? Some happiness mavens have argued that we're only as happy as we choose to be. If we're not happy, it means we've fallen down on the job. Not a very happy prospect. Now, brain science is coming to our rescue, with exciting new findings about neuroplasticity, the brain's ability to adapt and change. Pursuing happiness is not a moral issue but a practical one. Though we inherit a certain potential for happiness, we can enhance it by forming new neural pathways. With practices like meditation and cognitive training, we can reset our brains to experience the world the way naturally happy people take for granted.

Happy people see life as opportunity. Challenges are blessings in disguise. When we feel happy, our minds are open and expansive. Conversely, when we're open and expansive we feel happy. Happiness is an "upward spiral," as one researcher describes it. It makes us not only feel better but *be* better— better able to forge fulfilling relationships, find meaningful pursuits, and handle the vicissitudes of life. Happiness helps us stay healthy and whole no matter what the circumstances. Best of all, we can pass it on to those around us.

If you've picked up this book—or been given it by someone else—happiness is obviously on your mind. Maybe you're coming through a bad patch and wondering how to turn your life around. Maybe your life is pretty good but you think it could be even better. Either way, you'll want to explore what makes you happy. Finding answers means asking the right questions. That's where this book comes in. If you've thumbed through it, you've noticed the format is a bit different from most inspirational reading. There are twenty dialogues—hypothetical conversations—between a seeker and a wise friend. Each dialogue focuses on a quality or condition that impacts happiness, such as health, wealth, uncertainty, or time. At first glance, you may think the seeker's situation isn't the same as yours, so why would these exchanges have any relevance for you? Take another look. Behind the seeker's questioning lies the larger issue we can all relate to—the universal desire to be happy and to move past whatever is blocking us from reaching that goal.

The use of dialogue to inquire into our experience and find deeper meaning is a time-honored technique, famously used by Socrates, the Greek teacher whose student Plato faithfully recorded his dialogues. We've taken some liberties with the Socratic method; for one thing, the seeker poses most of the questions while the wise friend offers most of the answers. Maybe these aren't the exact questions you'd ask if you were in the seeker's shoes. But see if they point to something in you that wants answering. The wise friend just might speak to your concerns.

Happiness, it has been said, is the whole end and aim of life. But it can be elusive. We have to approach it indirectly, and with patience. Even then, we may not be sure what will be required of us. A teenager participating in an experimental program to prevent depression may have said it best: "People have the idea that being happy means skipping through the flowers. But happy is being happy with who you are."

THE WAY WE FEEL

How positive feelings can change your life

Happiness breeds happiness, and builds inner strength. Emotions like love, gratitude, and appreciation make us more expansive: we reach out to help others, and find creative solutions to problems. Good feelings are self-reinforcing. When we're happy, we can't help but flourish.

*Sometimes I feel like I'm on an emotional roller coaster,
reacting to whatever's happening around me. Any thoughts
on handling emotions? I'd give anything to manage anger
better, for example.*

> You and a lot of other people. Dealing with
> negative emotions—especially anger—is always
> a priority, but there's an even greater urgency now
> that we're living in such volatile times. We all know
> how destructive anger can be. It puts us at risk for
> major health problems, such as heart attack and
> strokes, and makes a mess of our relations with other
> people. All too often the response to anger is more
> anger, so conflicts rapidly escalate. If we want to
> promote peace in the world—even in our own little
> corner of it—we have to cultivate ways of
> transforming destructive emotions.

*Are you suggesting that it's better to suppress anger than
express it? I've never been clear. Bottled-up emotion seems
to have a way of leaking out anyway, but voicing anger only
seems to make the situation worse.*

> The prevailing wisdom used to be that it was
> healthier to express emotions, even negative ones.
> So there were a lot of people acting out in

destructive ways, and a lot of people suffering from the onslaught. Now the pendulum has swung the other way, and we know that expressing negative emotion can be a double-edged sword. Very few people are skillful enough to use anger constructively—as a tool to promote social justice, for example. Spraying anger around, as you pointed out, just makes things worse—not least because of what we now know from neuroscience. The brain is constantly being reshaped by our experiences and laying down new pathways. So if we're cruel, we're quite literally training our brain to respond with cruelty whenever our anger is triggered.

Does the brain do the same thing with positive behavior? If I repress my anger, for example, will I be less likely to act on angry feelings in the future?

Repressing an emotion isn't the same as consciously deciding not to act on it. As you've discovered, repressed emotion usually gets expressed, often in a backhanded way. But if, when anger, or jealousy, or fear arises, you are aware of what you're feeling and you catch the emotion before acting on it, then you are free to choose your response.

But how do I catch an emotion? By the time I realize what I'm feeling, it's usually too late: I've already reacted.

With emotion the challenge is that everything happens so fast; there are just microseconds between stimulus and awareness and, often, action. Paul Ekman, who's one of the foremost researchers on emotion, notes that our brains are set up so that it's not easy to interrupt the response mechanism or get rid of emotional triggers. For most of us the goal will be to recognize our emotions earlier in the game and learn ways to respond without overreacting. You mentioned anger. Say you're standing in line for a movie, and someone cuts in front of you. Some people will experience that simply as a minor irritation. But let's say you feel a flash of rage. Using various techniques you can train yourself not to lose your temper in that situation, and maybe even reduce the feeling it arouses to a twinge. But can you eliminate the anger altogether? Probably not—though the Buddhists would say that certain people can—and Western psychology is starting to think we have far more control than previously believed.

> ❝ He who lives in
> harmony with himself
> lives in harmony with
> the universe. ❞

MARCUS AURELIUS (121–180 ce)

How so?

Traditionally, Western psychology has held that all emotions—including negative ones—are part of our makeup, coded in the brain, so the best we can do is control our responses. The Buddhist view, however, is that destructive emotions are not part of our fundamental nature—which is pure—and therefore they can be eliminated. Granted, it takes years of dedicated effort by very experienced practitioners to get rid of negative emotions. But just knowing that emotions like anger and fear aren't permanent fixtures in the human psyche opens up the possibility of transformation and inner freedom.

How can I deal with negative emotions?

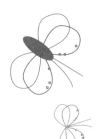

By becoming attentive to the workings of your mind and the feelings in your body, so that you are aware of emotions as they arise and can make choices about what to do with them. One way to increase awareness is through mindfulness practice. Research shows that mindfulness practice increases activity in the left cortex—the part of the brain that lights up when we experience positive emotion—reducing anxiety and improving concentration and mood. Ekman suggests we try to become more sensitive to other people's emotions so we won't jump to wrong conclusions about their intentions and behavior. The Dalai Lama's recommendation for cultivating empathy, as reported by Daniel Goleman in *Destructive Emotions*, is to start small, with ants and other insects. "Really attend to them and recognize that they too wish to find happiness, experience pleasure, and be free of pain," he says. From there, we can repeat the exercise with reptiles, then work up the evolutionary chain till we are developing empathy for human beings.

Why is it so important to cultivate positive emotions?

They're the key to happiness. Negative emotions narrow our focus—probably as part of our survival strategy—but emotions like joy, love, and gratitude do just the opposite. They rip the blinders off, giving us a much broader perspective on life. When we experience positive emotions we think differently, notes Barbara Fredrickson, a pioneering researcher in the field. As our minds open, we come up with new ideas and creative solutions. We also reach out to other people and become more giving. We want to help. A positive mood makes us more optimistic and resilient, enabling us to survive—even thrive in—difficult times. Feeling good not only makes us happy, it's life-transforming. "People who regularly experience positive emotions are … lifted on an 'upward spiral' of continued growth and thriving," Fredrickson explains.

But what if I'm not naturally optimistic? I can't just say, "OK, I think I'll feel grateful today," and expect it to happen, can I?

You can try cultivating positive emotions directly, by watching funny movies, say, or hanging out with upbeat friends. But what's more effective in the long run, according to Fredrickson, is to look for positive meaning in your daily life. Find the good in adversity, she says:

EXPRESS "APPRECIATION, LOVE, AND GRATITUDE, EVEN FOR SIMPLE THINGS."

A positive outlook isn't just personally beneficial; it can do wonders for organizations and even communities.

"A FOCUS ON GOODNESS CAN NOT ONLY CHANGE YOUR LIFE BUT PERHAPS ALSO THE WORLD, AND IN TIME CREATE A HEAVEN ON EARTH."

That's a far cry from what anger has been doing for the world of late.

A CARING HEART

How to cultivate compassion

When happiness seems elusive, remember the power of "please" and "thank you." A simple gesture of appreciation or generosity can turn someone's day around. Even our enemies deserve our gratitude: they teach us patience. We owe our lives to the kindness of others. Contentment comes from returning the favor.

Recently I took one of those trips where everything seems to go wrong. But every time I was ready to give up, someone—usually a stranger—would materialize and offer assistance. Such generosity couldn't help but lift my spirits. Now what made the trip so special seems obvious … kindness! That much kindness is unusual these days. Why do you think this is?

Kindness is one of the most undervalued commodities —which is too bad because, as you discovered, it doesn't take much of it to turn the day around. I wonder if we overlook kindness because it's so simple. What's really involved? Someone needs something, we help. Someone feels low, we console. Someone trips, we catch them. There's a need, we respond. Then the other person is grateful and relieved—and we're happy knowing we could help. Kindness is a low-effort, high-return exchange.

Sometimes being kind feels just as good as being on the receiving end—is that what you mean by an exchange?

Absolutely. The root of the word kindness is the same as that of "family"—or "kin." Kindness recognizes our kinship. In many cultures, the worst thing you can do is "dis" someone—show disrespect. Disrespect demeans, says the other person doesn't matter.

The message is, *You don't exist*. Kindness is just the opposite. You can't be kind without someone to receive it. Whatever form kindness takes, the bottom line is that you're making a human connection.

Some people seem to be naturally kind. But why is it that others really have to work at it, or never bother to try?

There could be so many reasons for sidestepping an opportunity to be kind. Maybe the person's simply having a bad day, or a bad year. The point is, it's never too late to learn. Charles Dickens' *A Christmas Carol* is a classic tale about this. After Scrooge is visited by the ghosts who show him the effect of his stinginess and the fate that awaits if he continues on that path, he vows to change. It might do us all good to be visited by the ghosts of our selfishness now and then.

❝❝ The greatest pleasure I know is to do a good action by stealth and to have it found out by accident. ❞❞

CHARLES LAMB (1775–1850)

But isn't kindness sometimes manipulative? I have an acquaintance who's always giving presents and doing favors. I can't help thinking, "What's the catch? What does she want in return?" Am I overreacting—or jealous?

> A little self-examination never hurts to see if you're measuring up to *your* standards, but don't compare yourself to others. Who knows why your friend needs to give so much? People with low self-esteem often think they have to buy people's love. If her behavior is interfering with your friendship, why not discuss it? Find a gracious way to say you appreciate her kindness but would like to leave it that in future you'll ask for help when you need it. Meanwhile, ask yourself if you ever use kindness for your own ends. Most of us do.

Sorry, I don't buy it. I don't go overboard like the woman I just mentioned. My sin is one of omission. Sometimes I just can't be bothered to extend myself. Then I feel bad.

> I'm not suggesting that we use some complicated calculus to factor kindness against rewards. But you've already noted that being kind has a payoff: it makes us feel good. And happiness is self-reinforcing. If we're happy in a situation, we're motivated to repeat it—and not just to be self-serving. The brain's

reward system has an evolutionary purpose: it encourages us to cooperate with one another.

So in A Christmas Carol *was Scrooge's payoff feeling better about himself, or feeling better because he regained friends and family?*

Don't you imagine it was both? Kindness breaks down barriers and draws people together. Scrooge was a late bloomer, but kindness and compassion generally begin to develop in childhood. Now and then you'll see an exceptional example of empathy in someone very young. I read about a young boy with cerebral palsy whose parents worked with the New York City public school system to create an innovative program integrating special needs children into regular classes. One of the boy's classmates was particularly sensitive and caring, becoming his devoted friend and protector.

When I hear a story like that I feel guilty. I'd like to do volunteer work, but I'm uncomfortable around people who are sick or have "special needs."

Kindness is kindness, but the way we express it isn't one-size-fits-all. Go where your heart leads you. My friend Lorna Kelly became very close to Mother Teresa in the last decades of her life. But when Lorna first

went to the Sisters of Charity mission in Calcutta, she didn't think she'd last the day—she had to bathe and bandage people with gaping, infected wounds. But some deep wellspring was touched, and Lorna not only stayed but revisited the mission many times. In her memoir, *The Camel Knows the Way*, Lorna writes, "In one way or another I believe we are called to do what Mother Teresa does—to be loving and to serve humanity in our daily lives in whatever form it might take: pastry cook, messiah, mechanic, emperor, housewife, poet, executive, saint, ballet dancer."

I don't see how just living my life shows caring. Running errands for my neighbor seems insufficient when there's so much need in the world.

The Dalai Lama points out that the word for compassion in Tibetan—*tsewa*—means compassion for oneself as well as others. That's why practices that cultivate kindness and compassion—such as repeating the Jesus prayer ("Lord Jesus Christ, have mercy on me") or doing *metta* (lovingkindness) meditation—can be so powerful. They help us feel part of humanity—not someone with more, or fewer, needs than others. When you wish happiness and well-being not just for those you love but also people you don't know and even those you don't like, you're increasing your chances of happiness and helping change the way we relate to one another. Sharon Salzberg, in her book *A Heart as Wide as the World*, points out that *metta* practice reassures us that we're never alone. While you're sending lovingkindness to others, everyone else doing this practice is sending it to you.

The Dalai Lama says, "My religion is kindness." What does he mean?
I can't speak for the Dalai Lama. But he often refers to a "basic spirituality" that isn't specific to any faith tradition but is grounded in what he sees as fundamental human qualities: kindness, caring, and compassion. In *The Art of Happiness at Work*, he sums it up as follows: "Be a good person, a kind person. Relate to others with warmth, human affection, with honesty and sincerity. Compassion."

The Dalai Lama is renowned for simple gestures that have a profound effect. He can be in a room with 5,000 people, but he'll notice the one person who's hurting and make a beeline for him. Sometimes he just takes someone's hands in his and gazes into their eyes and smiles or laughs. You can see their worry evaporate. At bottom, we all just want to be acknowledged, to feel that someone has noticed us and cares. He's a wonderful role model for that.

I'm intrigued with the idea of making a practice of being kind.

I think we're only just beginning to wake up to the power of gratitude and appreciation. If we did nothing more than say "Please" and "Thank you" to one another, we could begin to change the world. There's a wonderful TV ad showing two strangers. One woman has just inadvertently offended the other, and saying anything more will only make it worse. But suddenly she blurts out "Thank you!" to their mutual astonishment. The other woman's face changes from hostility to puzzlement to delight. They end up hugging. OK, life's not a commercial, but the point is valid: a simple "thank you" at the right moment can bring together two people who were poles apart. It's a startling simple idea.

Being kind and compassionate requires patience, the Dalai Lama points out. So, we should be grateful to our enemies: they give us the opportunity to practice patience. When Jesus said, "Love thy enemy," he wasn't suggesting self-sacrifice. He was daring us to take the fast track to happiness: being kind.

BEFRIENDING
THE UNKNOWN

How to be content with unpredictable outcomes

Often the future's a big question mark. That can be scary—especially if we're awaiting the results of a job application or medical check-up. But trying to predict outcomes, even those that might be life-changing, can sabotage our peace of mind. There are better ways to handle uncertainty and take comfort in the unknown.

Next week I'm having an engineering survey done on a house I hope to buy. I can't stop thinking about it. I keep trying to work out every possibility and to imagine my reaction if the survey turns up major problems. My heart's set on this house, but I'm driving myself nuts. How can I stop worrying?

It's a common problem—trying to second-guess the future, to taste it before its time. We want to live tomorrow's troubles today so we can put them behind us. We think we can anticipate all possible outcomes, but that's where we go off the rails. However carefully we plan, there's always the possibility that something will go wrong—and invariably, it's what we expect the least. You may think OK, it's an old house, so if there's a problem it'll be the furnace or the roof. Then you're thrown by the news that the foundation is cracked.

I like to think we have in our heads enough data to anticipate possible outcomes. But in a situation like this, where the outcome is uncertain, experience plus information equals ... well, in my case at least, it equals worry. Why do you think this is?

You're right to locate the problem in the head. Much of our anxiety comes from the brain make-believing it's half crystal ball, half computer. We delude ourselves into thinking we have the appropriate inner software to set the brain working on an impossible task: "Calculate all possibilities, then sort them in order of probability. Simulate the experience of the most probable outcomes, so I'll know what they'll feel like, if and when they happen." Now read my lips:

THE BRAIN HAS NO BUSINESS DOING THIS – IT ISN'T PART OF ITS JOB DESCRIPTION!!

But how can I tell my brain not to worry? I've tried, and it never listens. What should it be doing instead in its idle moments, when I'm riding the bus, or lying in bed waiting to fall asleep?

It would be great if we could brainwash ourselves into understanding that obsessive, speculative worry—as opposed to constructive concern—has never solved a single problem. It's like trying to play chess four moves ahead of your opponent: there are so many possible permutations of the outcome that even Bobby Fischer would be wasting his time on it. Of course, it's one thing to know this intellectually, another to accept it on a deep level. How can you just *stop worrying*—when worrying is what the untrained brain does by default?

Wait a moment, that's really interesting—the notion of the untrained brain. That ties in with my question, about what the brain should be doing in its idle moments.

Worrying was the brain's job a few million years ago. How else could we have figured out if those berries were safe to eat or that huge winged creature planned to have us for dinner? Now we can be reasonably sure that foraging in the supermarket won't kill us and that most predators are only figuratively out for our blood. Our day-to-day concerns have changed considerably, but our worry mechanism hasn't. It's up to us to reset the warning signals and red alerts.

When you put it that way, it seems obvious that instead of worrying, the brain should be reading, or writing, or planning, or creating— anything we were uniquely designed to do. But that still doesn't tell me how not to worry so much, at least about what I can't control.

Aye, there's the rub. How much do we really control? One thing we can't change is change itself. Everything

" Be patient toward all that
is unsolved in your heart,
and try to love the
questions themselves. **"**

RAINER MARIA RILKE (1875–1926)

is in constant flux, and we're powerless to stop it. Change—and death—are what we're really afraid of.

Afraid we'll lose what's precious to us?

Or that we won't get what we want in the first place. If you could control things to your liking you wouldn't be worrying about the engineering survey. You'd have maneuvered the situation in your favor already. Even when we don't know what we want, we know *that* we want. We're driven by desire. The Buddha said our unhappiness comes from wanting things to be different than they are. We worry our way into the future. Relief comes only from staying in the present. If you focus on this moment, this conversation, are you worrying? I thought not. In *The Wisdom of Insecurity*,

Alan Watts sums up our dilemma: "The brain is in pursuit of happiness, and because the brain is much more concerned about the future than the present, it conceives happiness as the guarantee of an indefinitely long future of happiness. Yet the brain also knows that it does not have an indefinite long future, so to be happy it must try to crowd all the pleasures of Paradise and eternity into the span of a few years."

Amen. If the survey goes badly, I'll probably be inconsolable. I could never find another house like this one. I'm not even sure I could stand the anxiety of house hunting again.

Sure you could. Because no matter how you feel when the survey results come in, you won't feel that way for as long as you imagined. Researchers have found we're notoriously bad at predicting the intensity of our emotional responses. Anticipation is a large part of any experience, and the brain knows this. It can rush in like an overprotective parent to shield us from anxiety, in the process spoiling our fun.

I've always been a worrier. Is this just my karma, or can I do something about it?

Even if you inherited a few more worry genes than your neighbor, you can still do a lot to retrain your mind. For starters, remind yourself that change and uncertainty are facts of life. Reframe your attitude, and you may even start to—don't wince—welcome the unknown. Mystery, like variety, gives spice to life.

"Welcome the unknown?" Not likely. I'm risk averse.

And proud of it, it seems. Pema Chödrön, a Buddhist nun with a very hip attitude, doesn't mince words on this subject. In *The Places That Scare You*, she says, "We can ask ourselves this question: 'Do I prefer to grow up and relate to life directly, or do I choose to live and die in fear?'" If you want to live a happy life, you have to dive in.

Could you be more specific?

Figure out if your fears are real, or you're fretting over what you imagine might happen.

Maybe I can't do anything about the survey. But if the deal goes through I'll have plenty to worry about—mortgage, neighbors, furnishings.

I said *real* fears. You'll have enough information to make those decisions in due course. You need to start living in the present and learn how to stop obsessive thinking. Whenever you catch your mind racing off, inwardly say, "Stop!" Be firm. Then turn your focus to something positive. Or try exaggerating your worry. Blow it all out of proportion, describe it in dire, life-threatening terms. It'll seem so absurd you'll end up laughing. Alternatively, you could schedule a regular freak-out—say from 5:00 to 5:10 p.m.—and postpone all worrying till then. You could also use mindfulness meditation to observe your thoughts, or a compassion practice to soothe your inner worrywart.

I don't worry so much when I'm really absorbed or feeling on top of things.

Competence gives us a sense of control. That's why learning a new skill or mastering something we once avoided feels so good. Post 9/11, we're all looking for some sort of hedge against insecurity. But all we can really do is tend to what's in front of us. Years ago, I saw a slogan that speaks to the senselessness of indulging in endless *what ifs*:

" People who live on the edge of a volcano understand the true meaning of life. "

EXPRESSING YOURSELF

How to court the artist within

How happy we are when we're creatively absorbed, dreaming up something new or re-imagining the familiar. Creativity is the fire of ingenuity that ignites daily life and illuminates a better future. We're all creative: the urge to shape and reshape the world is in our genes. Sometimes it just needs a little push.

I'd like to do something creative, but I'm not an artist.
If you're not born with talent, I guess you're out of luck.
Creativity isn't something we can learn, is it?

Let's start with your assumption that creativity and talent are the same. They're not, though many people confuse them. Talent is a specific inborn ability—a musical ear, say, or a knack for numbers. But even exceptional talent is only a potential until it's developed. That takes dedication, study, and practice, practice, practice. You're right in thinking that talent isn't distributed equally. For every budding Beethoven, there are thousands more who can barely hum a tune.

I CAN'T SPEAK TO WHETHER OR NOT YOU HAVE TALENT. BUT I CAN ABSOLUTELY PROMISE THAT IF YOU'RE ALIVE AND KICKING, YOU'RE CREATIVE.

Everyone's creative. It's an equal-opportunity genetic endowment.

So you don't need to *learn* to be creative. You already are. But if you want to express your creativity in a particular form, you'll need to make an effort to cultivate it. "Creativity is a habit," the choreographer Twyla Tharp tells us in *The Creativity Habit*, "and the best creativity is the result of good work habits. That's it in a nutshell."

Not very romantic. But it should help you put to rest the idea that creativity is some sort of mysterious ability you're lacking. When it comes down to it, creativity is about taking action. It's not just for artists. Anyone can be creative who is willing to commit to a creative process.

"Creative process"? What's that?

Everyone's process is different, but most people follow roughly the same path in turning a vague idea into a tangible result. Do you have something you want to make, a problem you want to solve, or a goal you want to achieve? We can take your idea and walk it through the process.

Well, I've been toying with the idea of putting together a family history. I've got photos and letters, some home movies, and my grandmother's diary.

Good. Your idea is to produce a family history. The first step is to explore your options. Gather every bit of information and material that might be relevant to your project. You're not making any decisions at this point, just checking out the possibilities. Assemble the materials you already have and check out sources for additional material. Consider possible formats: Should it be a book? A scrapbook with pictures? An oral history? A video or DVD? Go to the library, go online, talk with people who've created family histories. Research everything that's involved: the equipment you'll need, the time and money required, what kind of help you should enlist. Be thorough. The preparation phase is critical to the success of your project. It might take weeks or months, but it's worth every moment.

Once you've done all your research, let it "incubate." Turn it over to your unconscious. During this stage, many artists appear to be goofing off: they nap, meditate, do yoga, go for walks. One

> # ❝ Creativity is not the finding of a thing, but the making something out of it when it is found. ❞

JAMES RUSSELL LOWELL (1819-1891)

writer I know wanders through upscale department stores while a story is percolating. She's not shopping, just letting her mind drift in nice surroundings. Deep relaxation, dreaming, and the "twilight" state just before sleep are all highly conducive to creative insight.

At some point, you'll have an insight about your project. Make sure it's viable before you proceed. Let's say you suddenly realize that you unless you interview the older generation right now, while their memories are intact, the family stories will be lost. Since you have a camcorder, it makes sense to tape family members, then add other sound and existing visual materials, and create a mixed-media DVD on your computer.

The last stage involves putting meat on the bones of your idea so that it can walk in the world. This is the hard work of creating—what the inventor Thomas Edison meant when he said, "Genius is 1 per cent inspiration and 99 per cent perspiration." For you, this stage will involve many hours of taping, recording, editing, and mixing, until you have your family history packaged and ready to distribute.

The process you've just described is more or less what I already use in solving problems. I just never thought of it as creative.

What does creative mean to you?

Producing something totally original.

Originality is another aspect of creativity that's misunderstood. The early Greeks didn't think *anything* was original. Everything already exists as an idea, they said; creating art is a matter of intuiting those ideas and giving them concrete form. Many spiritual traditions consider creativity an expression of God. The artist is the channel; the product is almost incidental. Matthew Fox, a Dominican monk-turned Episcopal priest, describes creativity as "connecting to the Divine in us, and … bringing the Divine back to the community."

The divine gift you bring back to the community might be an artwork in the classic sense. But it could be anything you do with flair: raising a child, writing a report, making love, preparing dinner. Daily life is full of creative opportunities.

You make it sound like everyone's an artist.

Your life is your gift to the world—the ultimate expression of *you*. That makes it a form of art, with you as the artist. Not taking responsibility for our abilities, not living up to our potential is, to the creativity gods, our greatest sin. "Creativity causes the soul to rejoice," the mystic Meister Eckhart said. Creating is fun—even ecstatic at times. Children know this instinctively, but we need to be reminded that we're at our happiest when we're in the state of unselfconscious creative engagement that the psychologist Mihaly Csikszentmihalyi calls "flow."

Any suggestions on how to develop my creativity further?

Working artists treat being creative as a discipline. Discipline isn't forced labor, just structure. Routines and rituals ground us so ideas can fly. Twyla Tharp starts the day with movement—an early morning swim. Julia Cameron, whose *Artist's Way* teachings are the path-of-choice for countless aspiring creatives, religiously scribbles "morning pages"—three pages of stream-of-consciousness writing that clears the mind and catches ideas bubbling up from the unconscious.

CULTIVATE CURIOSITY AND INTEREST,

suggests Csikszentmihalyi.

TRY TO BE SURPRISED BY SOMETHING EVERY DAY.

Conversely, try to be surprising. Most creative people keep a notebook handy for brainstorms and observations. If you prefer images to words, you might keep an annotated scrapbook, as the photographer Peter Beard has for 40 years. Living creatively isn't for slackers. It means constantly working at your edge, challenging yourself to go farther.

Sounds like a lot of effort. What if I don't have the time or space for all that?

People who are serious about creating find a way to do it. They rise early or stay up late, sketch out ideas on trains and planes, turn parked cars or park benches into makeshift workspace. J.K. Rowling finished writing the first Harry Potter book in Edinburgh coffee bars. A commuter bus driver in New Jersey practices the cello in his empty bus during his lunch break.

True, some people—and some projects—require a dedicated space. (If you're painting 6x10-foot canvases, you'll want a studio.) Even more important is making *internal* space. There's a classic Zen story about a learned man who goes to a great Zen master for teachings. The master hands him a teacup and begins filling it with tea. The man keeps begging for teachings. The master keeps pouring tea. Finally, when the tea spills over the top of the cup, the learned man gets annoyed. Calmly, the Zen master says,

"YOUR MIND IS LIKE THAT CUP— OVERFULL. ONLY WHEN YOU'VE EMPTIED IT OF ALL YOUR IDEAS AND OPINIONS WILL THERE BE ROOM FOR WHAT I TEACH."

One of the biggest stumbling blocks to creativity is fear. Take up meditation and learn to concentrate so that you won't use fear—or life's inevitable distractions—as an excuse. Above all, develop your gift to the world. Whether your legacy is a child, a sonnet, or the best shortcake in the county, go after it with all your heart.

WHAT DOES MY LIFE SERVE?

How to do what matters

Why am I here? What should I do with my life? Happiness lies in your answer. A good life takes direction from the heart. Often it includes worthwhile work and contributions that outlast it. Purpose gives your path shape and direction. Having a sense of mission brings contentment. Fulfilling your mission is bliss.

Lately I've been feeling restless. Work isn't as satisfying as it used to be, and I worry about layoffs. I probably should find another job or even switch careers, but I can't seem to get up the energy to start looking. I keep wondering, "Isn't there more to life than this?"

Aren't you really asking, "Isn't there more to *my* life than this?" I can't help thinking of *The Divine Comedy*, Dante's epic poem about spiritual awakening. It opens with:

"Midway along the journey of our life
I woke to find myself in a dark wood,
for I had wandered off from the straight path."

Dante's pilgrim suddenly realizes he's lost his way—his sense of purpose. His nice, tidy life no longer makes sense. He's plunged into uncertainty. Today, we'd probably say the guy was having a midlife crisis.

It sounds as if you're going through something similar. You're no longer content with your life as it's been, but you're unsure of what comes next. From somewhere within you're being called to "something more." But what? You're tempted to pull the covers over your head and ignore the call, leave things as they are.

Sorry. That won't work. This is where the poet

Rumi might say: "The breeze at dawn has secrets to tell you. Don't go back to sleep." Don't lose the opportunity to step into greater awareness, to expand your possibilities. You think what you're looking for is a change of job or career, but I think you're engaged in a larger quest—redefining your life purpose and reclaiming a sense of meaning.

"Life purpose" sounds so lofty, so abstract. What does it really mean?
Life purpose is your focus, your reason for being, what gets you up in the morning. It's the answer to the question we all ask at some point: *Why am I here?* Purpose isn't a goal so much as the direction in which you're heading—your mission, if you will. Companies and organizations craft mission statements reflecting their principles and objectives, to guide their decisions and actions. Writing a personal mission statement is a useful exercise. You know you're not just your drives and desires. What, then, is your life about? What were you sent to Earth to do?

I'm not big on this "I-was-sent-to-Earth-with-a-mission" stuff. I'm more inclined toward "process theology": God set the universe in motion then left the rest up to us. Still, I want to think that my existence matters, that I'm contributing in some way.

The philosopher Bertrand Russell wrote a book, *The Conquest of Happiness*, in which he said he had concluded that people who view their life as a meaningful whole are happier than those see it as a string of events with no particular theme or direction. "Consistent purpose is not enough to make life happy," he states, "but it is an almost indispensable condition of a happy life."

Most of us, Russell notes, express our "consistent purpose" through our work. I suggest we define "work" in the broadest sense—as meaningful activity, not just paid employment. Let's say your purpose is to help people in grave need. Think of how many ways you could express it. You might have a job as a social worker, or a cabinet appointment as Secretary of Health and Human Services. Maybe you volunteer at a

&& The summit of happiness
is reached when a person
is ready to be what he is. ᴊᴊ

ERASMUS (C.1466–1536)

women's shelter, or lead a demonstration against the developer who wants to bulldoze the community garden to make way for a high-rise. If you're a celebrity, you might use your connections to raise large sums for famine or poverty relief. If you're Mother Teresa, you might run a ministry for the outcast and forgotten, and end up with a Nobel Prize. Maybe you're a full-time parent, raising a special-needs child.

Not surprisingly, our culture takes great interest in how work influences happiness. Researchers have found it's not *what* we do but how we do it that determines satisfaction. Whether they're CEOs or hospital orderlies, people who see their work as a calling are significantly happier and more fulfilled than those who treat it as merely the means to a paycheck. Even the amount we earn isn't as important as feeling that our work serves some larger purpose —and expresses what's in our heart. Nurses are leaving their profession in droves partly because they have to spend so much time on administrative tasks and monitoring high-tech equipment that they have no time for the one-on-one patient care that drew them to nursing in the first place.

What happens to people like those nurses when they leave their jobs? Do they lose their sense of purpose?

Losing your job doesn't necessarily mean losing your sense of purpose—unless your job is the meaning of your life. You can maintain a commitment to living a purposeful life even if the way you express it changes. People like Mother Teresa and Albert Einstein appear to have kept their life purpose and their work congruent throughout their lives. But for many of us that's not so. What drives your life at 20 isn't always the same at 30, or 40, or 50. What calls you to reassess your direction may be a crisis—job loss, health problems, a death or divorce—or simply the passage of time. Either way, a shift in focus often expresses itself as a career change.

I've been in the same field for years. I wouldn't know what else to do.

A place to begin is with the most basic question:

WHO AM I?

For centuries, spiritual teachers have instructed their students to meditate on that until an answer comes.

To speed the process, sit down with a pad and pen. Reflect on the question for a few minutes, then start writing. Let the words flow; don't edit yourself. If you need to prime the pump, explore related questions: *What are my talents, my gifts, my strengths? What do I love to do? What are the core beliefs that guide my life? If I could change one thing in the world, what would it be?* As you write, your purpose or mission may start to emerge, along with how best to express it.

The world of work has changed dramatically. We can no longer count on spending our entire career in the same company or even the same field. Questions about work satisfaction and life purpose are assuming new urgency. The call to awakening you received is a great gift.

What does the call to awakening have to do with work?

The word "vocation" comes from *vocare*, Latin for "call." The idea that work is a calling, that it has a sacred purpose, is very old. Something is lost when work is just an economic exchange. It can't help but be exploitive.

I'm drawn to work that's service-related. But that would mean a big salary cut. I'm really conflicted between wanting to do good and maintaining a certain lifestyle.

> You have to get honest with yourself. Want to find out what your priorities really are? Write your obituary. It's easy enough to answer the question: *How do I want to be remembered?* Now try the follow-up: *Am I living that way now?* Seldom can we get what we want in life without giving something up. Maturity is choosing the path to enduring happiness over immediate pleasure. Take the time to figure out what matters most to you now, then let that be the organizing principle of your life. Everything else will fall in around it.

I envy people who have a clear sense of purpose and never waver from it. What if I never have a flash of insight that says, "This is your true calling"?

> Not everyone has an epiphany. I've always liked what Rilke wrote to his young protégé: *"Live* the questions." If you give yourself fully to life, answers will come in due time. The Buddhist teacher Jack Kornfield is famous for his suggestion to spiritual seekers: Find the path with heart. Not bad advice for uncovering the theme of your life story.

MAKING
CONNECTIONS

How to nurture friends and family

Family, friends, colleagues, folks at the coffee bar or local pub—these relationships are what make life rich. "Only connect!" urged the novelist E.M. Forster. We'd be well on our way to lasting satisfaction if we spent more time cultivating community and less time at the office.

I'd like to see more of my family and friends, but I'm so busy just keeping my life going. How can I meet all my obligations and still give other people their due?

That's a pressing question for nearly everyone in our over-extended world. We talk a lot about shifting our priorities, but then the realities of day-to-day life intrude. As we juggle commitments at work, at home, and in the community, our nearest and dearest get short shrift. Often it's not until a crisis erupts—a spouse loses a job, an aging parent falls ill, a friend goes through a painful divorce—that we're shocked into realizing how much we've neglected the people who mean the most to us.

But you don't have to wait for disaster to open your heart. Start now. Consider the important relationships in your life. See which ones need attention.

Any suggestions on how to do that?

You could start by making a list of the people you're close to—family, friends, neighbors, colleagues. Then list the people who make your life, as it is, possible—doctor, dentist, babysitter, hairdresser, plumber, massage therapist, spiritual adviser. Go down the list and ask yourself the following questions:

DO I TAKE THIS RELATIONSHIP FOR GRANTED, JUST ASSUMING THAT THIS PERSON WILL BE THERE FOR ME? WHAT COULD I DO TO ACTIVELY NURTURE OUR CONNECTION?

After you've gone through the list, ask yourself:

WHAT WOULD I HAVE TO CHANGE IN MY LIFE TO MAKE MORE TIME FOR OTHERS?

We may have every intention of putting friends and family first, but when it comes time to act we find a

thousand excuses to maintain the status quo.
Behind most of those excuses is fear.

I'm afraid that if I cut back on work to spend more time with family, I'll lose my job. If I lose my job, the family will suffer. It's a Hobson's choice.

Losing your job is a common fear, especially if long hours are ingrained in your workplace culture. The message is: *Knuckle under, or you'll be passed over for promotion, or fired.* This is still a risk in the corporate world, but things are starting to change. With more people seeking work-life balance, even old-line employers are making concessions in order to hang onto good workers.

What if you went to your boss and simply laid out your needs, along with suggestions for how you could still contribute, if on a different schedule? You might be pleasantly surprised at the response.

Let's say your boss is fully supportive and lets you keep your job with fewer hours. Now you have more time for family and friends, they're bound to increase their demands on you. How will you handle that?

Mmm. I hadn't considered that. I'm used to being the one to decide when and where we get together. The question is, how can I make myself more available without turning into a doormat?

That's the tension in any relationship. To get close to others, we have to soften our boundaries. But we can't dissolve them completely, or we'll fall into co-dependence. Emotional boundaries are like the membrane around a cell—porous enough to allow an exchange of information, nutrients, and energy with neighboring cells, but strong enough to maintain the integrity of the individual. If you don't know how to protect yourself on an energetic level, you may find yourself feeling irritable or drained after being with certain people. Spending more time with others will give you an opportunity not only to deepen emotional bonds but also to create healthy boundaries.

How do you create boundaries?

One way is by learning to say no, without guilt or fear of rejection. If you're trying to cultivate a relationship, especially one you've neglected, it's tempting to be overly solicitous, even self-sacrificing. But you end up resentful, and the other person gets the message that you're a pushover. Undoing an exploitive relationship is a lot harder than making sure it doesn't develop in the first place.

Most of us are especially susceptible to the demands of children and aging parents. We want our children to be happy, and we feel a strong sense of obligation to our parents, who took care of us when we were young. But here, too, maintaining healthy boundaries is essential for building loving relationships. Children need boundaries to thrive; their sense of security comes from being held within safe limits.

But what about my parents? I can't turn my back on them now that they need me, but I'm uncomfortable with the way our relationship is changing.

No question, it's hard to watch our parents lose vitality and become dependent. After all, they're supposed to be consoling us. Without laying a guilt trip on yourself, see if you can treat them as you would anyone else in need. Have compassion for their feelings of helplessness and humiliation, their fear of infirmity and death. You might consider going on holiday together, or sharing a project that would bring you closer, such as putting together a family oral history or digital photo album. Set aside old hurts and resentments, and allow yourself to be fully present. This is your once-in-a-lifetime chance to give back to your parents.

I'd like to strengthen my connections outside the family as well. But people can be so thoughtless that sometimes it doesn't seem worth it.

It's true that people can be thoughtless, but they can also be generous and caring. One of the greatest challenges in nurturing relationships of any kind is accepting that we have no control over others. We have a hard enough time managing ourselves, yet we persist in thinking that if other people would do what we want, all would be smooth between us.

It's very useful to practice inquiring into the truth of a relationship, so that you can resolve any conflict between you. Think of someone who has angered, hurt, or disappointed you recently. Write their name on a piece of paper, then write why you feel the way you do. Be specific about what happened. As you reflect on the situation, ask yourself how you may have contributed to it. At first, you'll probably deny any

**❝❝ Come out of the circle of time
And into the circle of love. ❞❞**

RUMI (1207–1273)

responsibility; it's much easier to see how others have mistreated us than to acknowledge our own motives and behavior. But as you sit with the problem, you may begin to sense a subtle part you played—an ill-chosen word, a forgotten slight, failure to make your intentions clear. The moment you see your role, something switches, and the other side of the story comes into focus. The person you'd demonized becomes human.

OK, so I'm feeling less blame and resentment toward that person. But how does that make me want to reach out to others?

Once we acknowledge someone's humanity, we can empathize with them and feel compassion for their pain. We see that, like us, others are fallible and can be irritating and hurtful at times, but underneath, we share the same basic desire—to be happy. This is the central truth connecting us to everyone, everywhere.

When we truly grasp that we're connected to all beings, it comes as a relief. We feel free to reach out to anyone, friend or stranger. We have a sense of belonging in the world. We can take delight in our differences and, at the same time, take refuge in our own "tribe." When we can hold our own opinions without belittling others', everyone is satisfied.

THE CAVE AND THE POCKET

How to balance past, present, and future

We can never have too much time, but we can live too much in the past or the future. To find peace we need to strike a balance between remembering yesterday and imagining tomorrow. Neither regrets nor anticipation will spoil the present if you take inspiration from the image of the cave and the pocket.

I keep rehashing some dubious life choices I made years ago. When I'm not worrying about the future, I seem to be regretting the past— or wishing I could relive it! How can I stop harping on the past so I can enjoy my life right now?

Keep the past in a cave, the future beyond the horizon, and let the present loom so large you can't see beyond it unless you deliberately stretch to take a peek.

The past in a cave? That sounds a bit furtive.

Well, a cave's a marvelous place for hiding treasure. You wouldn't want to go there very often—the atmosphere's a bit dank and musty—but it's always good to know you've got something of value stowed away in there.

What's so valuable about the past? Isn't it just a lot of mistakes piled up like old logs?

Our memories are important because they trace a line of continuity through all the changes we experience. Rummage in one corner of the cave and you pull out a treasure—some happy time that makes you smile whenever you recall it. Poke around in another corner and you come up with a blunder—some wrong move that makes you wince. But even the worst mistakes needn't make you recoil if you remember the lessons you've learned from them.

What about the mistake I keep on making? The trap I've never learned to sidestep?

Take the mistake out of the cave. Shrink it down to a miniature facsimile of itself. Carry the image in your pocket as a talisman—a reminder not to give the error life again. Whenever you feel yourself falling into the trap, put your hand in your pocket and feel the mistake sharp and hard between your fingers. Let the gesture repel the looming error.

OK, I can see what you're saying about past mistakes. But what about past happiness? It can't be good to exaggerate happy memories either.

People who live in the past have made ghosts of themselves. Nostalgia's a vampire. Remember Miss Havisham, the embittered old spinster in Dickens' *Great Expectations*? Jilted on her wedding day, she still wanders about her gloomy mansion in her wedding dress, a prisoner of the past.

Brrr. That's a chilling image. So there's no happiness to be had in clinging to the past. But what about the future? Surely it's good to live in hope, isn't it?

Yes, indeed. "Hope is the cordial that keeps life from stagnating," the novelist Samuel Richardson said. Without hope we become either indifferent or despairing. Both are misguided. Indifference doesn't do justice to the precious blessings life offers, and despair easily spirals into self-pity or emotional paralysis. Without a doubt, hope is essential. Sometimes we feel overwhelmed by events and think nothing will ever change for the better. Hope keeps us going, even against all odds.

But beware: we should never use hope as a cushion against reality. It's OK for it to be an ingredient in our support system, but to lean on it too hard is to court disaster. False hope—believing that all will work out magically, without any effort on our part—is childish folly. To set our hopes too high is also a recipe for catastrophe. We all know what it feels like to be disappointed. Imagine the intensity of that disappointment when all your positive energy has been invested in hope, then things don't work out. Devastating!

But a moment ago you said it was OK for hope to be an ingredient of our support. What did you mean by that?

Hope directs our thoughts toward what's possible. It's "the thing with feathers / That perches in the soul," as poet Emily Dickinson wrote. People caught in situations that most of us would find utterly hopeless still manage to find meaning and joy in life. Theoretical physicist Stephen Hawking can neither move nor speak—he has ALS—but his unfettered mind never stops searching new scientific horizons. Actor Christopher Reeve, paralyzed in a horseback riding accident, became a passionate advocate for spinal cord research—as well as a role model for wheelchair-bound performers. Helen Keller transformed life for the blind and deaf.

Thankfully, most of us aren't faced with such extremes. How do we use hope as an ingredient of our support, and still do our part in creating the future?

All we can control really is what's going on right here, right now. Past and future balance on the fulcrum of the present. You've already seen how the image of the cave and the pocket can bring you forward from the past. And do you recall my suggestion to keep the future beyond the horizon and let the present

> **Real generosity toward the future lies in giving all to the present.**
>
> ALBERT CAMUS (1913–60)

loom so large you can't see beyond it without really stretching? Mindfulness practice is a way to reel yourself back from the future, so that the present looms large. Mindfulness simply means paying attention to your experience in the moment. Be aware of the feelings in your body and the thoughts going through your mind. Just observe your thoughts without following them anywhere or trying to control them. They'll move along on their own.

I'm starting to see that time isn't the enemy after all. It's my mind that gets me into trouble when it wanders off into the past and the future like a dog that's slipped its lead. So if I really try to focus on the present, I'll be a lot happier, no?

More like blissful, I should think.

Dialogue **8**

THE WISDOM OF LIMITS

How to be happy with what is

Even if we can't change the reality of a situation, we can choose our response. The wise know when to be proactive and when to let things be. When we stop trying to control life—and other people—doors open, miracles unfold, and the world is more hospitable. The path of least resistance leads to happiness.

I volunteer for a charity staffed by wonderful, committed people. But I'm becoming impatient with their resistance to new ideas. I have a lot of experience to draw on, but they keep stonewalling my proposals. How can I get them to see the light?

Isn't it annoying when we're sure we know what's best but others refuse to go along with our ideas? The more they oppose us, the more we push. The more we push, the more they oppose us. Stalemate. This is hardly the way to get anything done. No matter how right you think you are—and how misguided the other party—when you find yourself at a standoff, the message is clear: Stop. Do nothing. Something isn't working, and until you find a new

❝Seek not that the things which happen should happen as you wish, but wish the things which happen to be as they are, and you will have a tranquil flow of life.❞

EPICTETUS (c.55–c.135 CE)

approach, forcing your agenda will only make matters worse. Every problem has a solution, but when you're this polarized, no one can see it clearly. Accept the reality of the situation—that you can't agree—and you'll open the way for an answer to surface.

Even if I accept that we can't agree, it's not my nature to sit back and do nothing. Shouldn't I organize brainstorming sessions to encourage fresh ideas?

You just can't keep your hands off, can you? "Do nothing" means just that. There's a wonderful line in the *Tao Te Ching*:

"MUDDY WATER, LET STAND, BECOMES CLEAR."

If you stay still, without trying to rush in and clean up the mess, a situation can reach its own conclusion. This view is very alien to us can-do Westerners. In Japan, a decision involves gathering all the data, examining it from every angle, then allowing the best response to emerge. Here, we tend to project what *should* happen, based on similar situations in the past, and then make the current situation conform. You have a wonderful opportunity to practice accepting what is, and seeing what possibilities arise, rather than trying to bend the outcome to your will.

Are you saying that regardless of what's happening, we should accept every situation as it is? It seems to me there are times when being passive could have harmful consequences.

If a building's collapsing, don't wait for a consensus before you evacuate. But most of life is not an emergency. Accepting the reality of the moment is the logical starting point for change. Only when we know where we are can we see where to go.

I have a friend who's constantly dieting without success. I wonder if, in part, it's because she won't accept her body as it is.

Many people have the misguided notion that if they accept what is, they're conceding defeat. That's exactly the opposite of how acceptance works. When you acknowledge a situation fully, then you're free to make decisions and judgments about it. If the scale says 155 pounds, you can decide whether to diet or start exercising, or both, then set an attainable goal that considers your age, body type, and lifestyle.

So if I'm clear about what is, I should be able to change pretty much anything?

That's an interesting conclusion. By your reckoning, every woman, given enough will power and a little cosmetic surgery, could have a body like Halle Berry's. The Serenity Prayer says,

"GOD, GRANT ME THE SERENITY TO ACCEPT THE THINGS I CANNOT CHANGE, THE COURAGE TO CHANGE THE THINGS I CAN, AND THE WISDOM TO KNOW THE DIFFERENCE."

Acceptance requires us to consider all three, but wisdom is the crucial factor. Are you acting in harmony with reality, or willfully opposing it?

So is there some sort of test to determine what can or should be changed?

We tend to overlook the upside of acceptance: it triggers resourcefulness. "Fatalism is the lazy man's way of accepting the inevitable," novelist Natalie Clifford Barney said. The enterprising person sees the inevitable as a challenge: *How can I lead a good life within these limitations?* Anita Roddick's book *A Revolution in Kindness* introduces us to Herman Wallace, serving a life sentence at Angola, a notoriously harsh penitentiary in Louisiana. Wallace's prisoners'-rights advocacy landed him in a maximum-security punishment unit where the inmates were constantly attacking each other, physically and verbally. Looking for a way to ease tensions, Wallace had an idea: he organized a chess tournament the men could participate in while confined to their cells. The inmates made crude chessboards from paper, and as each pair of players called out their moves, the others followed along on their own makeshift boards. The result was miraculous. Animosity dissolved into friendly competition, and arch enemies began talking with one another. Significantly, it wasn't prison authorities but an inmate who came up with a solution. People who see possibilities in even the starkest reality can find happiness just about anywhere.

LIVING
YOUR TRUTH

How to find your moral compass

Your values tell your life story. What you do, say, think, and pray to speaks volumes about the principles that guide you. Where is true north on your moral compass? Whatever challenges you face, following your conscience can help you stay on the road to happiness. In the long run, it's character that counts.

Every day, it seems, I read about another politician or corporate honcho caught cheating, lying, or stealing. At work I see colleagues cutting corners, fudging results, goofing off on company time. At home I have to drum into my kids why copying their friends' homework is wrong. Even our governments and religious leaders can't be trusted. Are we in some kind of moral free fall?

It does seem as if there's been a dramatic shift in moral standards. But it's hard to know whether things are worse, or only look that way because more misbehavior is out in the open. With so many news sources today, nothing stays secret. What's good about this transparency is that it raises the bar—for individuals as well as institutions. We're all being taken to account for our behavior, our standards. Remember that old saw, "When you point a finger at someone, there are four fingers pointing back at you"? We're having to look at our own malfeasance: how we cut corners, fudge the truth, lie to ourselves and others. Events in the world are always a reflection of what's in the human heart. Seeing humanity's dark side confronts us with the less savory parts of ourselves.

> **" In matters of principle,**
> **stand like a rock;**
> **in matters of taste,**
> **swim with the current. "**

THOMAS JEFFERSON (1743-1826)

So when I see others doing something I don't approve of, I should keep quiet, since I'm not perfect either?

There may be misconduct you feel compelled to report. In some cases—such as child or spouse abuse—you shouldn't hesitate. But most of what we encounter falls outside the emergency category. Each situation must be weighed carefully. You wouldn't expose your firm for accounting fraud unless you were very sure you could back up your allegations—and were prepared to deal with the fallout. Similarly, you'd better have an ironclad case—and a very good reason—to expose a friend or co-worker for something that violates your moral code. From their perspective, they may be doing nothing wrong.

So morality is relative? What's taboo to me, or my family or culture,
might be acceptable to others, so we should just "live and let live"?

> We're seeing the consequences, even on a world
> level, of what happens when conflicting belief systems
> vie for the moral high ground and condemn other
> ways of thinking. Throughout history, black-and-
> white, good-versus-evil reasoning has led to conflict.
> Nearly every major religion has had its holy wars, with
> a few exceptions. The Buddhists and Jains have pretty
> consistently upheld their ethic of non-harm to all
> beings. Devout Jains even wear surgical masks so
> they won't inhale microscopic creatures. Living that
> way isn't for everyone, but the principle of reverence
> for life is something we could all endorse.

Are you suggesting that instead of getting my knickers in a twist
about other people's values, I should take a look at my own?

> No better place to start. Really examine the qualities
> or principles you value above all. Write them down.
> Does your list include qualities like loyalty, honor,
> generosity, courage, caring? Perhaps you lean toward
> the four cardinal virtues—prudence, justice, temper-
> ance, fortitude—espoused by Plato and, later, the
> Catholic Church. Maybe you uphold social justice—

freedom, equality, democracy, human rights. Your spiritual tradition may have a code of conduct you hold dear, such as the Ten Commandments, or the Buddhist precepts. What's your absolute bottom line—values you wouldn't go against for family, friends, or country?

I have principles I aspire to live by, but often I fall short. Truth is one of my cardinal virtues, for example, but I've been known to lie.

Nobody's perfect. Values are ideals toward which we strive. And truth, like most values, has many shades of meaning. There's truth as integrity—upholding your values in all you do. There's truth as right speech. Seldom do we tell the *whole* truth. Being brutally frank to others can be destructive, but we can never be too frank with ourselves. Truth involves seeing things as they are. We need to learn what truth means to other people, other societies. Under a totalitarian regime, "truth" is whatever those in power say it is—an abhorrent idea to anyone with democratic values. Recognizing how your personal value system differs from others' is essential.

I don't violate my moral code so much as compromise my values a little, here and there. For instance, gossip is on my list of don'ts.

Even saying nice things about someone who's not present makes me uncomfortable. But sometimes I can't even tell if it's gossip or not.

There can be a fine line between gossip and news. Some sociologists argue that non-malicious gossip is an important tool of social interaction—a way we bond with others and exchange information. But if it makes you uncomfortable, don't do it. You have that choice. Find a polite way to say you'd rather confine the conversation to people who are in the room.

Behavior that makes you feel guilty probably violates one of your core values. Just because other people are doing or believing something doesn't make it right—or right for you. Some people are exemplars of estimable values in some areas of life but complete cads in others. Think of the politicians who've dedicated their entire lives to public service while cheating on their wives. Conversely, you can do all the "right" things but for nefarious, self-serving reasons.

INTENTION MATTERS.

Now you seem to be saying that values aren't relative after all. Are there values we all share?

Nearly all societies condemn murder—unlawful killing. But then we turn around and justify the death penalty and war. Some societies sanction ritual killing of an adulterous wife or daughter. Even pacifists may condone "killing the one to save the many"—preventing a terrorist, say, from blowing up a building. Mercifully, most of the moral dilemmas we face aren't life or death. Every day presents us with countless small moments when our values are tested. Most of the time we're not even conscious of the moral calculus that drives our behavior.

Values are like the gyroscope in a plane. We continually veer off course, then our values make a correction. Clear values ensure a smoother ride. At the same time, we can't be so attached to our principles that we're unable to respond appropriately. When my best friend in childhood was stricken with diabetes and fell into a coma, she nearly died because her parents' religion forbade any treatment but faith healing. My mom whisked my friend to the hospital. She survived, and her parents dutifully administered the insulin injections she required. Ultimately, they forgave my mother and were grateful she had intervened. But you can see the risk involved, and how many different values came into conflict just in that one situation.

I'd be scared to intervene. What if the girl had died? The parents would have held your mother responsible, maybe even sued. Your mom would have felt terribly guilty. What can help us make weighty moral decisions?

We live in such litigious times that even doctors hesitate to get involved. But for many people, faith in a higher power or a strong sense of compassion gives them the strength to risk doing what they think is right. Most religions have rules or parameters that serve as a guide in making moral decisions. But even a moral code may not provide for every contingency. That's where prayer, mediation, and other centering practices come in. In connecting with the deep self and whatever divinity we believe in, we are guided to right action.

Values are immaterial if we don't embody them. They form the moral backbone that lets us stand up to the challenges of life.

TRUE RICHES

How much is enough?

We go to any lengths to earn it, win it, inherit it, spend it. Money is the answer to all our problems, we think. But is it? Are the rich happier? Would a windfall change your life? The truth behind the money myths will set you free. Real wealth isn't your bank balance: it's a feeling of abundance.

"Money can't buy happiness." How many times I've heard that. But having a little more would surely take the pressure off, at least. I'd like to pay off my debts and set aside something for the future. Don't a lot of other people feel this way?

> Money seems to be the number one concern of nearly everyone these days. If we don't have it, we worry about getting it. If we have it, we worry about keeping it. Families fight over it. Marriages are made—and dissolved—over it. Careers turn on it. Almost no one is dispassionate about money. And you're still convinced it would make you happy?

Well, a little happier anyway. A windfall or winning the lottery would be nice. On one of her TV shows, Oprah Winfrey gave a new Pontiac to each person in the studio audience. Don't you imagine those 276 people were pretty happy?

> Many were, no doubt. Others read the fine print and realized they had to pay taxes on the windfall. Some apparently had to sell the car to foot the bill. Let's get real for a minute. A windfall is no guarantee of happiness. A study of lottery winners found they were no happier than people who hadn't won. Furthermore, a disproportionate number of the winners have gone on to run up huge debts; a few

have even ended up in bankruptcy court. Sociologist Tim Kasser found that people who focus on money and possessions are actually unhappier than those who don't. Other research shows that, as we might expect, the poor are not as happy as people of even modest means. But once we've filled our basic needs, more money doesn't increase well-being. Over the past fifty years, the standard of living in America has doubled—yet life satisfaction has stayed the same. Even the super rich are only marginally happier than anyone else. The bottom line is that for all our obsession with money—getting it, spending it, saving it, investing it—having it has next to no effect on our happiness.

TRUE WEALTH ISN'T MEASURED IN ASSETS OR CASH FLOW BUT IN HOW ABUNDANT WE FEEL.

So if we're only as rich as we feel, what is wealth and what does it take to feel wealthy?

The Buddhist philosopher Nagajuna called contentment the greatest form of wealth. To Jacob Needleman, a professor of philosophy at San Francisco State University, "the only true wealth is a conscious life." Alas, many of us are unconscious about money. The subject is so fraught we tune it out altogether. But that only makes us susceptible to every siren song of our materialist culture. Remember when we were still reeling from 9/11 and President Bush said it was our patriotic duty to shop? Crazy as the suggestion was, it merely echoed the prevailing attitude:

"WHEN THE GOING GETS TOUGH, THE TOUGH GO SHOPPING."

Unfortunately, spending money to bolster our spirits, or—heaven help us—the economy, is an insidious form of self-destruction.

Where I get in trouble is in trying to keep up with other people. I overspend, then go into debt, and poof ... there goes my happiness.

Material values distort our thinking. We lose touch with the notion of real worth. To understand how value works, travel in a foreign country. When you're shopping in a currency that's unfamiliar, money comes unhooked from the valuation you're used to. You're forced to decide what things are worth by how much they're worth to you, not what's on the price tags. "Expensive" and "rich" are relative. You may feel flush when your year-end bonus raises your income to six figures, while someone else is crying poor with a net worth of $20 million. The deep root of the word wealth is "wish." Money always carries an element of longing.

I took my current job because of the salary. But now the pay doesn't seem like all that much, and I'm wondering if it's worth doing work I don't like just for the money.

Unfortunately, it's not always practical to follow our dreams. The new-age slogan "Do what you love and

" Not what I have but what I do is my kingdom. "

THOMAS CARLYLE (1795–1881)

the money will follow" holds out a false promise. Just
ask all the artists and writers who support their art
with mundane jobs. Money skews our attitudes
about work and vice versa. In *The Happiness Paradox*,
Ziyad Marar cites research showing that people with
volunteer jobs are less happy doing the same work
when they're paid for it. The majority of people have
no choice but to work for pay, but working strictly for
the paycheck is still, to most of us, soulless and
demeaning.

*If I took a job I enjoyed, it would probably pay less, and I wouldn't
be able to afford the things I need and want. What then?*

Then you'd have to ask yourself, *What do I* really
need? We're beginning to question our love
affair with "stuff." Research by Leaf Van Boven
and Thomas Gilovich suggests that people now
derive more happiness from experiences than

from things. "'The good life,'" they concluded, may be better lived by doing things than by having things."

But how do we really know how much is enough?

In *Nothing Left Over*, Toinette Lippe's memoir of a well-edited life, the author notes that for years she followed the familiar dictum

"LESS IS MORE."

Then she went to Cuba. There, she discovered,

LESS WASN'T MORE, LESS WAS JUST ENOUGH TO GET BY.

Lippe suggests changing the adage to

"LESS IS ENOUGH."

All we really need, she says, is "whatever is sufficient to deal with the situation we find ourselves in."

But "just enough" could mean a pretty meager life, couldn't it?

Maybe we're looking at this the wrong way—worrying about how much less we'd have instead of seeing what we'd stand to gain from having less to worry about. As Lynn Twist, author of *The Soul of Money*, points out, "When you stop chasing more of what you don't need, you free up tremendous energy to do more with what you have, and what you have grows." That goes to the heart of true prosperity. In *Your Money or Your Life*, the bible of the simple-living movement, Joe Dominguez and Vicki Robin offer a calculus for determining your real income by factoring in the life energy you expend on earning it. The bottom line is likely to come as a shock. Is the way you're living giving you the life you want? Many of us would have to say no. What we fail to grasp is that if we decided in favor of true wealth, we might have less money but end up with a much richer life.

THE PLEASURE CONNECTION

How to stir the senses

Beauty is more than just a pretty face. Thomas Mann called it "the only form of the spiritual that we can receive with our senses." Whether we find it in a person or a pair of shoes, a work of art or an act of courage, beauty brings pleasure that stirs the heart.

I've read that beautiful people are happier. Where does that leave the rest of us?

True, good-looking people seem to have the edge. Studies show they're more popular, earn more money, and are perceived as smarter, sexier, and more competent by parents, teachers, bosses, and lovers. But before you schedule an extreme makeover, consider carefully what else research has found: despite all their advantages, very attractive people are only marginally happier than anyone else is.

So if you're not a dead ringer for Nicole Kidman or Hugh Grant, relax. Turn your attention to what you love to do and want to achieve, and to cultivating close relationships. Because the other side of the equation is that people who are happy radiate beauty—the kind that doesn't depend on a chiseled chin or perfect nose.

So Mother was right—beauty comes from within?

Even some very attractive people think so. One pretty young actress recently told an interviewer,

"BEAUTIFUL PEOPLE OFTEN AREN'T PERFECT. YOU MUST HAVE A BEAUTIFUL SOUL, AND NO AMOUNT OF MONEY CAN BUY THAT."

Is beauty, then, in the eyes of the beholder, or are there standards everyone agrees on?

Philosophers and scientists have debated this question for centuries. But researchers now have identified certain features that people the world over find attractive. Symmetry is one. Think of the actor Denzel Washington—pretty universally regarded as a hunk. The right and left sides of his face are almost identical. Most of us aren't so lucky.

At the same time, we know from experience that what attracts us to other people has a personal component we can't always explain. There are things you or I find beautiful that others don't.

You mean, like my dog? He's a Shar-Pei. I look at him and see a kind of noble beauty; my friends just see a mass of wrinkles. But a dog isn't a Bach cantata or the Mona Lisa. *Wouldn't most people find masterpieces beautiful?*

Just because something is considered a great work of art doesn't mean that everyone finds it beautiful. What are the criteria you're using to judge it? The poet A.E. Housman contended that most of us, when we say we like a poem, aren't really responding to the poem itself—the stylistic elements—but to how it makes us feel. From that standpoint, we can see how notions of beauty might differ from culture to culture, neighborhood to neighborhood, individual to individual. What the Wolof tribe in West Africa finds alluring is very different from the standards used to choose Miss California. Even then, not everyone in California will agree with the judges' decision.

For me, beauty is connected to desire. When I see something gorgeous, I want to possess it, whether it's a pair of shoes, or a handsome guy.

Beauty attracts; the desire to possess is a natural response. But does it always lead to happiness? What if you can't have the desired object, or you get it but after a while, the thrill passes? It's like a beautiful scent—after fifteen or twenty seconds, you can't smell it anymore. Learn to appreciate beauty in the moment, without having to possess it, and you'll probably be happier in the long run.

But surely there are some beautiful things we never tire of, that continue to give us pleasure?

❝ Though we travel the world to find the beautiful, we must carry it with us or we find it not. ❞

RALPH WALDO EMERSON (1803–1882)

Nature is probably the best example of beauty that doesn't fade. It's self-renewing. Have you ever heard anyone say, "I'm tired of the sunset"? Every night it's different. Roses die, but the rosebush keeps blooming. Great art shares some of that same capacity to move us continually—if we're open to discovery each time we revisit it. Does it trigger a new awareness? Arouse a different feeling? Are you learning something new about the artist, or the medium, or the technique? Does it uplift you? The object stays the same, but your perception is always changing.

Poets and playwrights write endlessly about beauty, but they seem not to agree on whether it's ephemeral or lasting: "Beauty is forever"; "Beauty is short-lived"; "Beauty is immortal"; "Beauty will decay." What they don't dispute is its value, summed up in a poem by Ralph Waldo Emerson: "If eyes were made for seeing, / Then beauty is its own excuse for being."

"Beauty is truth, truth beauty," the poet John Keats famously wrote. Fashion is deliberate artifice, a thumb in the eye of the status quo. But true beauty is honest; it has integrity. Fashion shocks. Beauty awes.

What's wrong with fashion? Wearing pretty clothes makes me happy.

The question is, are they clothes you truly find beautiful, or what the fashion industry tells you is attractive this season? For some people, getting dressed is an art form. But when clothes are mere "trifling amusements"—to borrow a phrase from Aristotle—their effect is likely to be short-lived. Styles change. For the ancient Greeks, beauty—and happiness—were moral issues. Amusement is not happiness, Aristotle warned. It's the "nobly beautiful" that moves us to make virtuous choices.

"Virtuous choices" don't sound like much fun. How do they make us happy?

It's a matter of perspective. The author John O'Donohue, an Irish Catholic priest, has pointed out that *how* we see determines *what* we see—which, in turn, affects our happiness. Do you find beauty in many places, or just a few? Some people walk right by a beggar on the street without noticing; others see the beggar, think "ugly," and avert their eyes; still others see someone beautiful—a fellow human being struggling to make the best of life. Mother Teresa was known for looking past the disease and deformity and utter degradation of the destitute she ministered to in the streets of Calcutta, and seeing each person as the child of God. "The graced eye can glimpse beauty anywhere," O'Donohue writes in *Beauty: The Invisible Embrace*. "When we beautify our gaze, the grace of hidden beauty becomes our joy and our sanctuary."

Is that what beauty is for—to call out our compassion, make us aspire to be better people?

That's one possibility. Beauty in the realm of spirit is not about pretty surfaces and pleasing forms: it's about experiencing a transcendent force—even death. John O'Donohue says that helping someone die is the most beautiful gift we can offer. I wonder if the greater gift isn't to those who remain behind and bear witness. Dying is the great mystery, our deepest

A few days before my father died, he withdrew into a coma. Then one morning, he suddenly sat straight up in bed, gazed into the distance and with a rapturous look on his face declared,

" It's so beautiful! "

before falling back on the pillow. Two days later, he was gone. But I had the distinct feeling that he had already moved on, toward whatever unearthly beauty had beckoned from beyond.

fear, the passage that all beings, without exception, must make. To stand at the threshold as someone slips through the door is to glimpse beauty in the midst of sorrow.

So beauty can bring us solace when we're suffering?

In challenging times, keep something beautiful in your heart, suggested the French philosopher Pascal. This simple but profound prescription has sustained innumerable people imprisoned in one way or another through the centuries. Hiding in her attic in war-torn Amsterdam, Anne Frank wrote: "Think of all the beauty ... in everything around you and be happy." It's an idea that could serve us anytime.

Science has now found that positive and negative feelings reside in different parts of the brain. Happiness is not just relief from suffering but something we can cultivate. Rather than trying to blot out bad feelings or sorrow, we can dose ourselves with beauty to jump-start the healing process. Whether as an image, or a scent, or a sound, beauty is encoded in our sense memory. We can carry it like a talisman—a reminder of the radiance that fills the human heart.

Dialogue **12**

MAKING
IT LAST

How to have a happy relationship

Loving another truly is one of life's great joys.
For ongoing happiness, nothing matches a
relationship that excites, enriches, and uplifts.
Here, we plumb the mystery of love, from
the thrill of desire to the rewards of lasting
partnership. Intimacy has challenges, too:
we discover the true meaning of doubt.

*Love is one thing, commitment another. What's the secret
for making a relationship work long-term?*

Everyone has qualms about intimacy and
commitment at some point. That's the paradox of
love: we yearn for a relationship that will consume
us, body, mind, and soul, then when we find it, we
worry we'll get *too* close and lose ourselves. Forging
a strong and lasting bond that allows both of you to
thrive is a delicate process. The first thing to remember
is: *Take your time.* Intimacy can't be rushed.

*Point taken. But if I'm having doubts, should I even be considering
a deeper commitment?*

Most people take doubt as a sign the relationship isn't
working. But in a relationship that's still unfolding,
doubt often signals just the opposite—that you
already have gone deeper and are feeling vulnerable.
Fear naturally arises when we reveal another, more
intimate layer of self. Each veil we shed brings us
closer not only to the one we love but also to our
own essential core. Until we're comfortable with this
deeper level of intimacy, we may continue to throw
up a defense against the fear. Doubt, or ambivalence,
is one form it can take; anger and jealousy are others.

If we're not aware of what's behind those feelings, we're likely to assume that the problem is the relationship or our partner, and that the only solution is to bail out.

OK, I can see how doubt might be a positive sign that the relationship is going deeper. Still, how can I tell if love is lasting? Maybe this is nothing more than infatuation and sexual attraction.

Romance isn't one thing, sexual desire another, and the urge to settle down together still another. All are stages of love. Granted, the feelings at each stage differ. They're triggered by different parts of the brain, each producing a different chemical, according to anthropologist Helen Fisher. Each stage has a distinct role in the process of pairing up. Sexual attraction and romance are what draw us together and keep us interested as we move toward intimate commitment.

We all come to relationships with expectations. Some, we're not even aware of. Often these agendas don't surface till the glow of romance starts to fade. Suddenly the person you fell in love with disappears. You face a choice. You can cry "Irreconcilable differences!" and split up; many love affairs end at this point. Or you can decide to put your differences (and your disappointment) in perspective and see what you can learn from one another. Intimacy is a great teacher. The beloved is a mirror continually reflecting back to us what we cannot—or will not—see: our kindness and compassion, our pettiness and greed, the truth of what we really want. If you can view your partner's quirks and flaws as small parts of a much bigger picture, you'll have a base for building a relationship that brings lasting happiness.

So you're saying I should just ignore what I don't like about my partner?

We all know that doesn't work. Feelings arise. You can't control them, but you can choose your response. Say you and your partner are decorating your first home by combining the furnishings from your former dwellings. The problem is, you can't stand his taste. But you want the place to be comfortable for you both, so you're highly motivated to find a solution. He agrees to discard some of his stuff, and you think of ways to incorporate the rest in a harmonious scheme.

Creating a harmonious relationship is a similar process. Just as you don't love all your partner's lamps and chairs, odds are you won't love every stick of his *interior* "furniture"—his beliefs and habits. But if you can make the relationship your priority, the differences between you will start to seem more superficial and less threatening. You may even find room for a fishing trophy or two.

Another way to handle your partner's "otherness" is to reframe it in a positive light. Imagine that your partner is an exquisitely wrapped present you've just been given. You tear off the paper in anticipation, open the box, and find that it's filled with smaller boxes. Some of these boxes contain valuable items; others, small trinkets. You don't love all the gifts equally, but the whole package is so original, so fascinating that the one or two items you don't like hardly matter. If you can think of your lover as a precious gift, you won't be so disappointed if he doesn't live up to all your expectations.

But doesn't everyone have expectations? And wouldn't someone who truly loved me want to meet my needs, just as I'd want to meet theirs?

If we think that the purpose of a relationship is to satisfy our needs for sex, companionship, security, and family, then living up to our expectations will be key. The brain in love secretes chemicals that make us feel happy, more outgoing, and more productive. But research shows that winning a video game or eating chocolate also fires up the reward centers of the brain. Something more than a rush of good feeling from having our needs met is involved in love that lasts.

Some spiritual traditions hold that love is the path of transcendence and union with God. Just as love breaks down the boundaries between you and your partner, it dissolves your sense of separation from the divine. Many Eastern philosophies teach that everything, everywhere is spirit; every love affair, then, is a form of worship, a prayer. The 13th-century Sufi poet Rumi wrote poems of devotion to God, but he could just as easily have been addressing an earthly partner:

**❝ Oh, my Beloved!
Take me,
Liberate my soul,
Fill me with your love ... ❞**

That's beautiful, but my "beloved" is pretty down to earth. I can only imagine the reaction if I said our relationship was a path to God. Do you have any practical suggestions to bring us closer?

Everything we've discussed is practical, whether it's developing self-awareness, especially about your expectations, or focusing on what's precious in your partner. Above all, be patient. Don't give up on each other or the relationship too soon.

Half of today's marriages end in divorce. But studies show that marriage continues to be the greatest source of happiness for most people. We divorce because we can. There's less need to hang in and see if problems can be resolved with time. But couples who opt to stay together rather than divorce often are pleasantly surprised to find that a deeper, more enduring relationship emerges.

Obviously, you shouldn't stay in a relationship that's physically or emotionally abusive, or empty of love or caring. But at the other extreme, quitting too soon robs you of a prime opportunity to work through self-defeating behavior patterns, develop inner strength, and learn the true meaning of love.

"The true meaning of love"? Explain.

Most of us cling to a romantic view of love. We expect the passions of courtship to last forever. We forget that love isn't something we *have* or *feel*, but something we *do*. In committing to someone "for better or worse," we agree to actively participate in creating a caring, supportive partnership—and not to bolt whenever we're restless or bored.

Ask any long-married couple if they've ever had doubts. If they're honest, they'll tell you about times they nearly separated—or did—and a thousand other times they felt angry, or hurt, or full of regrets. But they'll also tell you what sustained them in tough times: the sex, maybe, or separate vacations; their faith, or their children; a sense of humor, or a foundation of trust and respect. True love includes all that.

THERE'S NO FORMULA FOR FINDING HAPPINESS OR LOVE THAT LASTS. EACH PERSON, EACH COUPLE MUST ARRIVE AT THEIR OWN CALCULUS.

THE POWER OF HUMOR

How to lighten up and live

Humans and apes are the only animals with the capacity for laughter. Why waste such a precious gift? A good laugh can make us healthier, happier, more productive, more at ease. Shared laughter forges friendships and fosters goodwill. In uncertain times, laughter is our saving grace.

People tell me not to take life so seriously. But there doesn't seem to be much to smile about in the world today. How can I lighten up?

You're right, the world's a mess. Sometimes our lives are, too. But wringing our hands does nothing to remedy the situation. Unless we learn to see life as a divine comedy, we'll find nothing but tragedy wherever we turn. There are problems we need to address, individually and collectively. But to be truly effective we must discriminate between what we can change and what we can't. A sense of humor helps put things in perspective.

I remember laughing a lot when I was younger. What happened?

Children laugh, on average, up to 300 times a day, adults just 17. Obviously, age is a factor. Most kids don't have the worries or responsibilities we have. Plus, we're more discriminating about what we find amusing. But clearly you're not alone in your concern. There is now so much scientific evidence of the physical and emotional benefits of humor that a whole industry has sprung up around it. You can now get laughter therapy, laughter yoga, laughter clubs, laughter coaches—there is even a "laughter ambassador training" program and several scientific and medical associations. Put "laughter" in your search engine and you'll see what I mean.

I do laugh when I'm happy. But when I'm not, very little amuses me.

It's true, happy people laugh more. But the principle behind laughter therapy is that you can laugh your way *to* happiness and health. The physical act of laughing can actually lift your mood. According to pioneering psychologist William James, we don't laugh because we're happy so much as we're happy because we laugh. Twenty minutes of laughing exercises in the morning can set up your body and mood for the day.

"Laughing exercises?" You must be kidding. How could I laugh at nothing? Even if I could, how would it improve my health and mood?

Robert Provine, a pioneer in laughter research, shares your skepticism. He contends that laughter evolved as a social signal, not "a calisthenic for body and soul." But we've come a long way from our ape cousins. Even if geletology—the scientific study of laughter—is still a young field, it doesn't mean that we should dismiss all the findings. You can always check them against your own experience.

> **"** Real religion is
> the transformation of
> anxiety into laughter. **"**

ALAN WATTS (1915–73)

For starters, laughing is good stress relief: it can dissolve irritation and anger. It also calms anxiety. Laughing relaxes our muscles—hence the expression "weak with laughter"—and can lower blood pressure. It blocks stress hormones such as cortisol and adrenalin that cause wear and tear on the system. One of the most important claims for laughter is that it stimulates the immune system to produce cells that fight disease and tumors. That in itself would make it worthwhile to cultivate a sense of humor.

Laughter also triggers the release of endorphins—the brain's natural opiates—which make us feel good and feel less pain. The "laughing yoga" folks claim that like certain *asanas*—yoga poses—laughing massages internal organs. It's also good aerobic exercise.

> SOMEONE CALCULATED THAT IF YOU LAUGHED UPROARIOUSLY FOR AN HOUR, YOU'D BURN MORE CALORIES THAN IN AN HOUR OF WALKING.

Laughter is natural cosmetic surgery: every time you laugh, you're toning 15 facial muscles. And the good news on the work front is that people who laugh a lot are demonstrably more creative and productive, not to mention happier than their colleagues.

OK. I get it. So what are these laughing exercises I'm supposed to do?
Hanging out with funny people is an obvious place to start. You could also watch funny movies or TV comedy shows. Clinical interest in laughter and healing grew largely out of Norman Cousins's use of comedy to help reverse the effects of ankylosing spondylitis, a

painful degenerative disease. Cousins was a well-known magazine editor when he received the dire prognosis. With his doctor's OK, he checked out of hospital and into a hotel, where he watched tapes of Marx Brothers movies and the TV show *Candid Camera*. "Ten minutes of genuine belly laughter ... would give me at least two hours of pain-free sleep," he wrote. After Cousins published an article about his experience in the prestigious *New England Journal of Medicine*, interest in the healing power of laughter really took off. Cousins later said he thought any positive emotion, not just laughter, could aid healing. Nonetheless, having a sense of humor about life remains one of the most direct routes to happiness.

If you're not into comedy, you could spend 20 minutes a day practicing laughing. Take a few slow, deep breaths, then as you breathe out, make a HA-HA-HA sound (use HE or HO, if that's the sound of your natural laugh). Keep repeating until your diaphragm muscles are contracting rhythmically and the automatic laugh response kicks in. Then you're off and laughing. If you get bored, make silly faces. Open your eyes and mouth wide, and stick out your tongue: in yoga, this is known as Lion pose.

If you can't seem to generate a good laugh on your own, consider joining (or forming) a laughter club. A number of groups have web sites that include laughing exercises and instructions on finding a group. Laughing groups build on the idea that we laugh more with others than when we're alone. That dovetails with Provine's theory that laughter is a social signal—an auditory wink to anyone who's listening.

I'm a social laugher. Even when I read something hilarious, I seldom laugh out loud. I get more joy out of sharing a laugh with friends.

Laughter draws us together, no question. The people who measure these things say that only 20 percent of the time is our laughter in response to a joke. More often we're exchanging anecdotes or stories, or laughing at something in our immediate environment.

Laughter is more than tension relief. It's a major tool of interpersonal—even international—diplomacy. Used strategically, laughter disarms. A shared laugh can defuse a tense situation, cut short an angry exchange, and make us more conciliatory. Wasn't it the entertainer Victor Borge who called a smile "the shortest distance between two people"?

But sometimes laughter is cruel, isn't it?

True, laughter can be a form of one-upsmanship. Sarcasm and biting humor are aggressive forms of this. Dorothy Parker and the Algonquin Round Table used their wit to devastating effect. Healing laughter, however, is inclusive, not divisive.

A lot of humor turns on incongruity and surprise. Something happens, then the response isn't what we expected—it doesn't follow logically—so we laugh. Many spiritual traditions use humor of this sort to awaken students. Zen masters are particularly adept at humor that forces you out of your mind and into your heart. This is also the intention of the court jester and the holy fool. The jester plays the buffoon, but he's the only courtier allowed to tell the king the truth. The holy fool is another "simpleton" whose message is, in fact, profound. The Sufis use hilarious teaching tales about the wily fool Nasrudin to prick the self-importance of the conditioned mind.

So laughter can be spiritually transforming?

That may be its most important role. Humor cracks open our narrow, self-obsessed thinking, making room for a more enlightened, more expansive view.

Dialogue **14**

HAVING IT YOUR WAY

How to be a happy achiever

Success, it has been said, is getting what you want; happiness is wanting what you get. We can't always get what we want, but does that mean we have to settle for less? Here, we learn how to be happy and successful. The secret is defining success in your own terms.

I set goals, I work hard, and I achieve them. To most people, I'm a success. But whatever I accomplish, it never seems to be enough. What will it take to feel satisfied?

There are several issues here. Let's start with the feeling that whatever you accomplish, it's not enough. The question is, what's "enough"? And by whose standards are you measuring it?

In our culture success seems to mean having a good job, money, power, fame, and a loving family. My life's pretty good, but when I look around, I see people with so much more.

What you're saying reminds me of that old gag line: *Just when I think I've reached the goal, they move it.* We forget that *we're* the ones who keep moving the goal, not the culture or other people—not some external force that's beyond our control. If we're victims of anything, it's our own mental tendency to fix on certain conditions we think will make us happy and then pursue them. When we succeed, all's fine for a while. We've got the job, the house, the car, the spouse, the portfolio, status, so we feel good. But before long, things start to go stale. Work is no longer challenging, the boss is a tyrant, the house and the car are too small, and we don't have enough money to support the lifestyle we think we deserve. What was "enough" no longer is. We want more.

One explanation for this drive toward "more" is a phenomenon called adaptation. The brain has a built-in tendency to become accustomed to stimuli, so that after a while, we no longer respond to them. Whatever turned us on before becomes the "new normal" and stops giving us a lift. When we can't get a happiness fix from what used to make us feel good, we look around for something else.

You make wanting to be successful sound like an addiction.

For some people, it is. Success becomes a kind of addiction when we stop focusing on *what* we're going after and start worrying about the lift we'll get from it. But like any "high," this kind of success is only temporary. To feel the adrenalin rush, we have to continually find something new to aim for and achieve, continually get another shot of acclaim. Pursuing success becomes a vicious circle. We're never satisfied.

This chronic dissatisfaction, chasing after the next new thing, is what the Buddha called *dukkha*. We all experience it to one extent or another; it's the human condition to want. But there is a way to break out of the vicious circle of desire and dissatisfaction. Mindfulness practice—observing our grasping tendency as it arises, without acting on it—is one method. Nearly every spiritual tradition offers some form of relief.

Are you saying that in order to be happy, I have to forget about success?

The point isn't to forget about success, but to look very carefully at how you define it. Whatever we tell ourselves success consists of, fame and fortune are still at the top of most people's list. It may surprise you, therefore, to learn that in most dictionaries, the first definition of success makes no mention of fame or fortune. Success is simply "a favorable outcome"— the achievement of something tried or planned.

OK, so I define success in terms of money and recognition. But why shouldn't I want to have nice things? And don't I deserve recognition for my achievements?

There's nothing wrong with wanting recognition or nice things. But your question was how to be both successful and happy. I'm suggesting that as long as you tie success to externals—earning a lot of money,

> ❝ Our greatest glory is not
> in never falling but in rising
> every time we fall. ❞
>
> CONFUCIUS (c.551–479 BCE)

owning expensive toys, maintaining a certain image—your happiness will always be at the mercy of forces beyond your control, whether it's the fluctuations of the stock market, changing fashions, or your boss's mood.

But if you view success as an inside job, you'll be able to achieve a kind of success that is its own reward: the self-esteem that comes from knowing you can set goals and follow through. You might gain riches and recognition in the process, but your happiness won't depend on it.

What do you mean, "success as an inside job"?

In other words, success based on your own, not society's, values. What activities or accomplishments make you proud, even if no one's watching? They don't have to be monumental to anyone but you. In a recent magazine article asking women to identify the biggest success of their lives, the responses ranged from quitting smoking to graduating from medical school at age 48. A friend of mine, who's not very mechanical, considers it a triumph whenever she makes a minor repair around the house. To anyone else, replacing a shower head would be insignificant, but in her mind, she's a star.

Each of us has our own measure of success. There will always be a handful of high achievers who count nothing short of writing a bestseller, or qualifying for the Olympics. But the rest of us, if we look closely, can find our lives full of winning moments: running a marathon, sticking to a diet, learning to drive a car or a golf ball, painting a portrait or the kitchen, celebrating an anniversary, or ending a relationship without blame or rancor. Both Princess Diana and Jacqueline Kennedy Onassis considered raising happy children the pinnacle of success. The billionaire businessman and philanthropist Ted Turner—a man of diverse achievements—shares that view. "There's no way you can be successful in life if your children aren't successful," he told a TV interviewer. To Bessie

A. Stanley, winner of a 1904 essay contest, success was "to know even one life has breathed easier because you have lived." Maybe your greatest accomplishments won't make the nightly news, but they will give you something far more enduring—self-respect.

So you're implying that if I want to be happy, I should count my blessings?

That's one way to put it. You could make a gratitude list—what's working in your life, what's turning out for the best. Those are all successes. Or you could take a closer look at where in your life you're investing the most effort, and see if it's giving you an *inner* payoff. "Success makes life easier. It doesn't make living easier," the rock musician Bruce Springsteen said. I think what he meant is that no matter how rich or famous you are, you still have to cope with your feelings and responses.

Sometimes I think I was more successful when I was younger.

A lot of people feel that way: "I was such a high achiever in grade school. What happened?" It's not success per se that changes: it's our expectations. When we're young, we get recognition for things like good grades, popularity, and athletic prowess. Later on, as life becomes far more nuanced and complex, so do our requirements. We might have different standards of success for different domains: work, creativity, love, health, fitness, charitable endeavors. And there are times in every life when success comes down to something basic: surviving an illness, overcoming a setback, learning from a mistake.

In truth, no achievement is too humble to be a source of happiness. The Stoic philosopher Marcus Aurelius said it best:

> ## "BE SATISFIED WITH SUCCESS IN EVEN THE SMALLEST MATTER, AND THINK THAT EVEN SUCH A RESULT IS NO TRIFLE."

DRAWING ON THE SOURCE

How to tap sacred strength

Faith transcends religion or creed. It's a force available to all, regardless of beliefs. Think of it as an open line—a 24/7 connection to sacred source. It guides us to a true path and friends along the way. Strong faith brings happiness. We feel at home in our lives and in touch with something larger.

I've read that people with strong faith lead happier lives. But these days, beliefs seem to be another excuse to fight. How can faith be a key to happiness when we're so intolerant?

We need to make a distinction between faith and belief. To quote the late Alan Watts, author and Zen pundit: "Belief is the insistence that the truth is what one would wish it to be. Faith is an unreserved opening of the mind to the truth, whatever it may turn out to be." Belief is about doctrine and dogma: every religion and sect has its own take on what's true. Beliefs define the differences between us, which is why they're so divisive. Faith, on the other hand, is universal to all humans, irrespective of beliefs. Interfaith scholar Raimon Pannikar calls faith "a primal anthropological act." Everyone has faith in something, religious or not.

❝ Faith is to believe what you do not see; the reward of faith is to see what you believe. ❞

ST. AUGUSTINE (354–430 ce)

But when people refer to "my faith," don't they generally mean their beliefs—their religion or spiritual practice?

There *is* a relationship between faith and beliefs. As Fenton Johnson, an ex-priest in both the Catholic and Buddhist traditions, explained in an interview, "our beliefs ... provide a home in which and through which we may sustain and develop our faith." Organized religion isn't the only home for our beliefs, or the only vehicle for nurturing our faith. Some 90 per cent of Americans say they believe in God or some spiritual force, yet less than half of them attend regular worship services. People whose beliefs and practices fall outside the traditional forms often describe themselves as "spiritual, but not religious."

Whatever gods and goddesses we pray to, whatever ultimate principles we meditate on, to really understand faith we have to move past sectarianism to the level of source. Physicist-theologian Ian Barbour says faith "refers to a man's ultimate trust, his most basic commitments, what he bets his life on, the final basis by which he justifies all his other values. The religious question is precisely about the object of a person's devotion; it asks to what or to whom a person gives his ultimate allegiance." In her book *Faith*, Sharon Salzberg, a Buddhist teacher, notes that in Pali, the language the Buddha spoke, faith, trust, and confidence are all translations of *saddha*—literally, "to place the heart upon." Faith is not something we have, she says, but an action we take. When we "faithe," we leap into the unknown with confidence.

Confidence in what? Sounds more like the proverbial "blind faith."
Faith is blind only if you choose not to see—not to verify truth for yourself. It's easy to be dazzled when we discover a spiritual teacher or teaching that seems to hold the key. Buddhists call this "bright faith." It inspires us to make the spiritual journey, Salzberg points out, but it can become blind faith if we accept everything at face value.

But isn't the whole point of faith that we accept the unseen and unprovable without question?
And look where that's led the Catholic Church in recent years. Doubt is an essential part of faith, Salzberg says. You need to consider carefully where you place your faith, then test the teachings to make sure they're relevant to your life. Even if you've held

the same beliefs for years, it pays to hold them up for review now and then. If you develop trust in what Salzberg calls "your own deepest experience," neither complacency nor charismatic messages will seduce you off the path.

What's to prevent me from being misled by my own experience?

Anyone can be deluded. That's why it's good to check out any "messages" or revelations from on high with a spiritual advisor, or submit them to the test of time. On the other hand, we're so conditioned to think that only our religious leaders have a direct line to timeless wisdom that we don't realize that our own firsthand experience is our best defense against self-deception. Remember the tale of the Emperor's New Clothes? Only the little boy would admit that the emperor was naked. Imagine if that kid had doubted his eyes! So it is with spiritual matters. Once you've checked things out for yourself, you're no longer in the realm of belief. You *know* what's true for you.

Some years ago, I drove to a Zen Buddhist retreat with a senior executive of a pharmaceutical company. One of the other passengers asked him why he practiced zazen, *a rigorous form of meditation aimed at direct experience of spiritual awakening. "I'm not interested in belief in God," he said. "I want to see God."*

By connecting us to our own inner experience, faith points us toward what's real. Not just in spiritual matters but in every sphere of life.

I still don't see how having strong faith makes us happier.

It gives us meaning, security, a sense of belonging, for starters. Spend a Sunday at a church in Harlem—it's often an all-day affair with a huge potluck meal after the service—and you can't miss the power of spiritual community. "Religion" comes from the Latin *religare*, to bind back. Faith links us not only to ourselves and our spiritual allies, but to the vast web of being. Here, everyone is welcome at the feast, without ethnic, political, or religious distinctions.

Isn't that a little idealistic, considering the state of the world?

Idealistic, or optimistic? Faith has to do with trust in our better instincts, and the hope that we'll make saner choices in the future. Science has confirmed what we've long suspected: optimists are happier, pessimists more realistic. But cultivating an optimistic outlook is not some crazy form of denial. It may help save us. Faith gives us the stamina to tackle problems and reclaim the shadow—those denied or repressed aspects of self and society that, like unloved children, strike out and wreak havoc. We have to develop spiritual intelligence.

What's spiritual intelligence?

What we've been talking about—the perspective that puts timeless values above selfish striving. Spiritually intelligent people have wide-angle, long-range vision. They approach life with humility.

Sounds good, but is it practical? How can faith help me where the rubber meets the road?

Faith is infinitely practical. Psychologist Mihaly Csikszentmihalyi says in *Good Business*, "At this point, good business depends to a large extent on the same values that undergird the major religious traditions." This doesn't mean religious domination of the workplace—just bringing soul to those institutions that claim so much of daily life. Replacing the dog-eat-dog ethic with values like decency, generosity, integrity, accountability, and respect would change the way business operates and make us happier, healthier, more motivated workers.

Pastoral counselor Sharon Parks describes faith as "the ongoing weaving of the fabric of life—giving

> ## ❝ The prayer of the heart is the source of all good, refreshing the heart as if it were a garden. ❞
>
> ### ST. GREGORY OF SINAI (d.1360)

form, order, pattern, cohesion, and holding power to disparate elements of experience." It can't guarantee you a promotion, or get your kids into college, but it can move you to see your life as meaningful. Oprah Winfrey's magazine, *O*, ran a story about an order of nuns who all had been successful professionals before ordination. Now they support themselves by selling cheese made from their cows' milk. If made with love, the cheese "will speak," the mother superior told writer Sara Davidson. "Everything we make that goes out of here speaks. That's one way contemplatives speak to the world."

Everything *you* do speaks as well. Faith puts the words in your mouth. The question is: Do you know what your life is *really* saying?

KEEPING THE PEACE

How to find your still, calm center

Life today is so hectic, with so much
information coming at us, that our biggest
challenge is maintaining inner calm.
Sometimes what it takes to be happy is to
slow down and listen for the voice of truth
within. There we find what T.S. Eliot calls
"the still point of the turning world."

My neighbor is totally unflappable. She seems to glide like
a swan over the surface of life while I'm paddling furiously
just to stay afloat. I envy her calm. What's the secret to that
kind of composure?

Some people are adept at maintaining an unruffled exterior, regardless of their inner state. They're like those actors whose effortless performances belie hours of preparation. We love to be around people like your neighbor because they keep their angst to themselves. They don't make emotional demands on us, and the calm they project is very soothing. To cultivate this quality in yourself, you'll need to develop your own strategy for maintaining inner balance. You and your neighbor may be worlds apart in temperament. Following your own path rather than imitating hers will bring you more contentment in the long run.

My so-called path is pretty scrappy. Forget meditating: I don't have
the time or discipline to do it regularly. Then I get mad at myself for
being so weak-willed. How can I ever find serenity if I can't even
sustain a simple concentration practice?

Whoa. Listen to your language and all that self-judgment.

> STEP ONE TOWARD SERENITY IS TO TREAT YOURSELF WITH UNDERSTANDING AND COMPASSION.

Pretend you're your best friend. What would you say to her?

For starters I'd confess that I don't really relate to meditation. For me, the most effective way to chill out and center myself is to move— yoga, tai chi, tennis, dancing. Something like Gabrielle Roth's 5 Rhythms™—ecstatic trance dance— is perfect: I can hook into the music, work up a sweat, and work off stress—all at the same time.

See? You're not undisciplined or weak-willed. It takes commitment to do the practices you mentioned. Be careful not to judge yourself against some imagined standard—you'll only add to your stress. For every person who finds meditation soothing, there are others who swear by playing the piano or going to the movies.

I keep hearing about work–life balance. Whatever it is, I don't think I have it. I work hard and keep long hours. I love what I do, but I feel guilty when I read those magazine articles saying I should be spending x number of hours a day with friends and family, x number on "me time," or whatever. Is this something else I should worry about?

Every self-help guru seems to proffer "rules" for how to lead a balanced life. Ultimately, each of us has to write her own prescription. When my sister ran a bed-and-breakfast, she had a guest who spent eight months of the year working on the Alaska pipeline and the rest in my sister's garret, writing novels. That's certainly not a conventional definition of a balanced life, but it worked for him. Lives skewed toward work are commonplace today. Balance for you may just mean making sure you eat right, sleep enough, and have a few tricks for de-stressing during the day. They don't have to be complicated. My favorites include ducking into a church or an art museum during my lunch break, or gossiping over coffee with a friend.

The worst threat to my serenity is information overload—all those emails, not to mention the junk mail and the phone calls hawking

financial services and real estate deals. How can I stay calm in the
midst of all this "noise"?

Fortunately, there are ways to stem the flood
of junk mail and phone calls; you can research
them online. A lot of people I know have stopped
reading newspapers and are cutting back on other
media coming into the home. Reducing the
information flow will certainly help make your life
more tranquil, but I'd hate to see you eliminate
news sources altogether. Now more than ever, we
need to be intelligent, informed citizens. And the
problem isn't really what's going on outside. We
can't turn the volume down on the world—or
even on our noisy neighbors, much of the time.
We have to come to terms with our surroundings
on an inner level. The road to serenity always leads
back to ourselves—and to not fighting the truth
of our lives.

So serenity comes with self-acceptance?

Trying to be what we're not or live in ways we can't
sustain prevents us from being at peace with
ourselves. Sometimes serenity is as straightforward
as feeling at home in your own skin.

The Power of Yes and No

Saying yes to what feeds you emotionally and spiritually is essential for inner peace and well-being. Saying no to what drains your energy or pulls you off center is requisite for inner balance. Make your "yes" and "no" lists. Post them where you can seem them easily—by the phone, perhaps—and update them frequently. They'll serve as an instant reminder whenever you're tempted to stray from your commitment to serenity.

WHOLE-PERSON HEALING

How happiness affects wellness and vice versa

Are happy people healthier? Are healthy people happier? The relationship between health and well-being is well established. But how does this bond work? And how can we make it stronger? A variety of strategies— from nutrition and fitness to a positive attitude and forgiveness—can help us heal.

Flu season's coming, and I'm a little nervous. Last year, I got sick and couldn't seem to get back on my feet. My spirits plummeted, and the more depressed I felt, the worse my physical symptoms seemed to be. This year I want to maintain a healthy attitude so I won't get sick. Any suggestions on how to stay upbeat and well?

What seems like a simple question is really quite complex. You're obviously aware of the connection between attitude and physical health. And you've discovered that illness affects how happy you feel. So it should be no surprise to you that health is one of the factors people mention most often when they're asked what influences their happiness most. Researchers don't know whether good health makes people happier or if being happy makes people healthier. Either way, happiness appears to be a healing force. A sense of control over forces impacting your life is another factor in both happiness and health, so let's begin answering your question by determining which you feel is more directly in your control—your happiness or your physical health.

I was about to say "my happiness," because I'm constantly hearing that happiness is an inside job. But I realize that there are also a lot of things I could be doing to improve my health. I guess I should consider health first.

Do you have any pressing health issues—any ailments or concerns? It may be something lifestyle-related, such as weight control or balancing your diet. Maybe it's a condition that impacts major body systems— high blood pressure, say, or high cholesterol. Or perhaps you have a chronic complaint that affects your sense of well-being, such as herpes, or chronic fatigue syndrome.

HEALTH, AS YOU KNOW, IS A WHOLE-PERSON MATTER. A BREAKDOWN IN THE SYSTEM MAY EXPRESS ITSELF IN ONE SYMPTOM OR ANOTHER, BUT SYMPTOMS AREN'T THE DISEASE.

When we're not feeling well—particularly if we're experiencing a kind of vague, general malaise—we need to explore a bit and see where we're under a lot of pressure. Stress contributes to just about every illness you can think of.

I've been reading some books about the metaphysical causes of various ailments. One says, for example, that psoriasis is linked to emotional insecurity and multiple sclerosis to rigid thinking. Do you think this sort of analysis is helpful?

I'm glad you said "helpful" rather than "accurate." I'd be wary of anything other than a diagnosis by a licensed healthcare professional that claims to know the "cause" of an illness. Causality is complex, and so far medicine has not found many links between specific attitudes or emotions and specific conditions or diseases. I question relying on metaphysical practitioners to make diagnoses. Where those "readings" may help is in giving you another perspective on your condition. People who are very attuned to their own bodies often self-diagnose with surprising accuracy. And sometimes highly intuitive people pick up on our unconscious awareness and confirm information we didn't know we knew.

One reason I feel better in the hands of alternative or complementary health practitioners is that I don't feel so powerless. Holistic healers don't talk down to me—unlike many doctors I've seen—and they seem to regard treatment as a partnership that only works if we work on it together.

Assuming an active role in our treatment makes the healing process faster and more effective. The medical system—particularly managed care—seems to strip of us our dignity and power. All too often the medical team treats us as if we're incapable of making any decisions about our health care. Happily, medical training is beginning to stress the importance of good doctor-patient relations, and more doctors are encouraging their patients to be proactive and informed. A big step toward feeling happy and whole is to take back the reins in your health care.

I'm pretty good at getting the right care when I'm sick or injured. What I'm not so good at is preventive care. What's the first step?

Where do you think you're most vulnerable? If your diet isn't healthy, you might want to consult a nutritionist and find an eating plan that takes into account your food preferences as well as your metabolism. Ayurvedic medicine is interesting in this regard, as it looks at nutrition in the context of your whole system—your *dosha*, or body-mind type. Maybe your diet's okay but you're not getting enough exercise. Here, too, a holistic approach can be helpful, to fit exercise together with your other fitness goals and find activities you'll stick with. All the good intentions in the world are of no use if you don't follow through. You might hate low-impact aerobics and drop out after a few sessions but find that you enjoy water aerobics so much that you sign up for an extra class each week.

I DON'T KNOW WHY WE DON'T REALIZE THAT "FOLLOW YOUR BLISS" APPLIES TO HEALTH AND FITNESS AS MUCH AS TO WORK, CREATIVITY, AND THE SPIRITUAL PATH. VIGOROUS

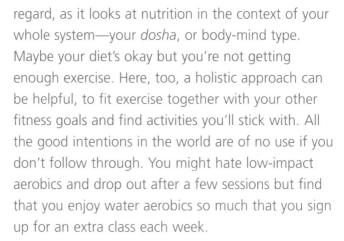

EXERCISE FOR JUST TEN MINUTES RAISES ENDORPHIN LEVELS FOR AN HOUR. THAT'S AN EASY HAPPINESS FIX.

When I'm not feeling well, though, I don't have the will to pick up and do any of the healthy things I should. What then?

If you're feeling a little depressed, push yourself past your resistance; even mild exercise has a lasting effect on mood. If you're overstressed or dealing with chronic pain or illness, consider something like Mindfulness-Based Stress Reduction. Based on mindfulness meditation and relaxation, it has impressive science behind it and is excellent at reducing discomfort and improving your mood. Many busy people go to the other extreme and ignore illness to the point that it jeopardizes recovery. Again, I can't stress enough the importance of listening to your body. Learn its subtle vocabulary. You'll be amazed what your symptoms will tell you about your physical and emotional needs. That's where those metaphysical equivalencies can be useful: if you have a stiff neck for no apparent reason, ask yourself "what's a pain in the neck to me right now?" Maybe something is bugging you—a person at work, a project you're resisting. The symptom is a way into your deep psyche—to your hopes and fears, wishes and concerns. The solution may be as simple as forgiveness. Letting go of resentment and forgiving others is one of the most effective paths we have to health and happiness.

> **"** He who has **health** has **hope**, and he who has hope has **everything. "**
>
> ARABIAN PROVERB

NATURAL WONDER

How Earth's infinite mysteries delight

What is it about gazing at the stars or watching pets at play that makes us supremely happy? Some of us climb mountains in search of the sublime; others find pleasure pottering in the garden. The natural world is at once infinitely mysterious and marvelously simple, reminding us of our place in the great web of being.

*Whenever I'm feeling out of sorts, I instinctively head out the door.
I only have to walk along the beach and hear the seagulls cry to feel
that everything's going to be all right. How come Nature makes me
feel so totally alive and content when nothing else can?*

We could probably find all sorts of reasons why we
respond to nature. But I wonder if the rapport you're
describing isn't something deeper—a spiritual
"coming home." Nature puts us in touch with the
essential self and, ultimately, with God. Sufi poetry
is shot through with natural images for this sacred
relationship—the orchard, for example, represents
worldly existence—and the garden's symbolic role
figures large in many traditions. Today, however, we
don't seem to have much in common with Nature.
We barricade ourselves behind glass to protect
ourselves from the weather. We dress up our
dogs in coats and booties, and treat them more
like pampered children than animals. Whether
we're distancing ourselves from Nature or
anthropomorphizing her, she resolutely remains
"Other." She follows her own laws, oblivious to ours.
We may burn Nature, cut her, try to trample her into
extinction, but somehow she pops up again and

prevails. That untamable quality inspires both fear and admiration. Nature is utterly unsentimental, so we're left to project our romantic notions onto her.

That makes Nature sound rather distant, forbidding. I find the natural world awesome, even overwhelming, at times: the wind and ocean during a hurricane, say, or those technicolor sunsets you see out West that take my breath away. But personally, I get more pleasure from an intimate relationship with Nature.

You're not alone. Gerald Manley Hopkins wrote a wonderful poem that starts off,

"GLORY BE TO GOD FOR DAPPLED THINGS— FOR SKIES OF COUPLE-COLOUR AS A BRINDED COW; FOR ROSE-MOLES ALL IN STIPPLE UPON TROUT THAT SWIM."

These words always remind me of an old pied horse pastured on a farm near where I grew up. He certainly didn't inspire awe, and I wouldn't have called what we had a spiritual connection. I just liked him because he listened. He was the perfect audience: utterly unjudgmental and unable to give feedback or advice. Most of us are so talked out. Words dominate our days. How utterly refreshing it is to form relationships that consist of touch and snuggling, and long periods of companionable silence. Animals offer that.

If only I could be so open and trusting with people! *I found myself telling someone the other day that I was going to stay home over the weekend to spend some "quality time" with my cats. They're feeling abandoned, I explained, because I've been out so much. But how do I know that's how they feel? I could just be reading something into their behavior because I want so much to think we're really communicating.*

It's uncanny how much animals seem to sense and how responsive they can be. Research has pretty much established that animals are highly intuitive, and now there's speculation that they can understand the meaning of our words, not just the feeling behind them. Of course, we probably won't ever really know what animals are thinking. Nature is the great mystery. No matter how many of her secrets we crack, more remain. That's part of her intrigue, don't you think? She's the veiled woman, the dance-away lover. I'm reminded of Lilith, fiercely independent "she-demon" of Hebrew myth said to have been Adam's original consort, before Eve. Nature at full throttle clears away whatever is dead, damaged, or superfluous, to make way for new growth. In doing so, it reflects "this quality of Lilith's to instinctually, with fire and passionate heat, cut to the essential nature of things," Jungian analyst Barbara Black Koltuv explains in *The Book of Lilith*.

So is it possible that mountain climbing, deep-sea fishing, and extreme sports are a way guys respond to this Lilith force of Nature?

Could be, though I doubt they're thinking in those terms. There has always been a streak of "noble savage" romanticism running through our relationship with the natural world. We like to test our mettle, use the wilderness as a kind of pumice to scrub us down to our inner wildness. City dwellers often get a special charge out of back-to-nature visits. There's nothing like the thrill of stumbling on a lek—the communal mating display characteristic of certain birds. An encounter like that makes us feel

> ## " A heavy snowfall disappears into the sea. What silence! "
>
> ### ZEN FOLK SAYING

we've been able to string a rope bridge across the divide between ourselves and the elusive Other.

How can people who genuinely love Nature go hunting or fishing?

There's a big difference between killing for sport and either culling—killing a certain number of animals to maintain the ecological balance of a region—or taking animals for food. It could be argued that if you kill in a fully conscious state, there's some respect for Nature in the act—at least an understanding that She's not our servant but our co-equal in the great web of being. Alas, I haven't met many hunters who think that way. Most are hell-bent on showing Nature who's boss. It's this refusal to see ourselves as inseparable from Nature, or at least in partnership with Her, that environmentalists blame for the rape of Earth's resources. For complex reasons people in impoverished or developing areas are sometimes forced to use

natural resources in unsustainable ways. But wealthy societies like ours have the luxury of choosing how we relate to Nature—and often we don't choose wisely. Anyone who truly wants to see animals up close in the wild can take up bird-watching, or "tracking"— following animals' tracks to observe them undetected.

What about the nurturing aspect of Mother Nature?
Whenever I see wheat fields or cows grazing, I'm reminded of nature's fecundity. It's awesome to think that Earth produces all this abundance for us to enjoy. Well, maybe not just for us, but we're the major beneficiaries.

You're right, Nature's abundance is not all for us. We weren't even around for the first 100 million years or so of her glory. Now we're making up for lost time, stripping off whatever we can of her bounty. We're like drunken sailors on shore leave, bullying our neighbors into giving us their resources, as if we have to consume as much as possible before the ship sets sail again.

As for Nature's gentler side, even city folk who've never seen an apple on the tree or heard a coyote howl tend their house plants and pets with great care and affection. Granted, there are extremes. There's now a web site ostensibly for arranging doggie play dates, but as you might guess, it's really a dating service for pet owners, not their pets.

Still, Nature in some form is a near-universal source of happiness and contentment. Roger Scruton, a contemporary British philosopher, suggests that there could hardly be a more blessed existence on Earth than that of a dairy cow in its lush pasture. Landscapes have provided inspiration and pleasure for millennia. Perhaps no one has celebrated the enlightening capacity of Nature as fully as the Chinese. Vistas that have since been destroyed by industrialization once gave rise to luminous scroll paintings reflecting the timeless truths of the *Tao Te Ching*:

TAO GIVES ALL THINGS LIFE
TE GIVES THEM FULFILLMENT
NATURE IS WHAT SHAPES THEM
LIVING IS WHAT BRINGS
THEM TO COMPLETION.

VITAL
RECALL

How to create happy memories, starting now

Do you reminisce about the good times? Do you wallow in "if onlys"? Memory is slippery. Sometimes it tells us what we want to hear, sometimes what we need (but don't want) to know. To lay down happy memories for the future, live fully in the present. Then, however things turn out, you'll remember you did your best.

I keep thinking of Edith Piaf's famous lyric, "Je ne regrette rien."
My father said the same thing—though in my opinion, he had plenty
to regret. I want to remember the past truthfully. How can I
guarantee that someday I'll be able to say, "I regret nothing"?

The short answer is, make sure you're really living now. Strictly speaking, life is nothing but memory. Except for what's happening this second, we only know our experience in recollection. What we think, say, and do become the memories that make up our ongoing life story. This is the tale we tell ourselves and others— full of facts, we assume, but inevitably some fiction. My guess is that your father wasn't implying he was happy about everything he'd done. No life is free of pain, loss, and disappointment. Rather, I suspect that, like Piaf, he had dined heartily on life's banquet and was satisfied he'd left no dish untouched. If you're alert to the possibilities in every situation, even if you screw up royally, you won't be left with the bitter taste of regret. Be open-minded, take risks, and expand your horizons, and you should have more than enough happy memories to entertain you in old age. That's what all those "ten-things-to-do-before-I-die" lists are about—having no regrets.

Back up a minute. What do you mean that our memories inevitably include fiction? I thought the whole point of memory was to remind ourselves what really happened?

Oscar Wilde called memory "the diary that we all carry with us." It's the faculty that enables us to recall events. What we recall is not the diary, but the entries in it—the memories. We have this notion that valid memories are fixed and unchanging, and that remembering simply means recalling the facts. In reality, memory is slippery—highly subjective and suggestible. Our memories change as we change and begin to see facets of the past in a different light.

That makes me a little uneasy. If memories aren't firm, how can we tell what's real? How do I know I'm not just inventing my past— rewriting it however I see fit?

None of us can be sure our recollections are factual. The brain records all we experience, but memory has a habit of editing, rearranging, and embellishing the narrative as it reconstructs it. I've always loved Lily Tomlin's line—"reality is nothing but a collective hunch." Memory is like that. Certain events are burned into the collective psyche. We agree that World War II was fought, and that hijacked planes flew into the World

Trade Center and the Pentagon on September 11, 2001. Extraordinary events are more firmly imprinted in the brain and more easily recalled. We pay closer attention when they happen, and they trigger a lot of associations and emotions. But even when there's universal agreement that something has occurred, our individual interpretations of it will differ—often widely.

What about happy memories? Aren't we more likely to recall details of the good times—a wedding, a job promotion, going on holiday—than the bad?

We hope so, which is one reason we snap pictures of such occasions. Thirty years later the wedding album will trigger fond memories of that day—unless, of course, you've since divorced. Whether memories are happy or not depends not only on how you felt at the time, but also on your current perspective. "The most faithful autobiography is less likely to mirror what a man was than what he has become," biographer Fawn Brodie noted. Most of us would rather dwell on happy times than painful ones, so we try to forget or erase bad memories and cling to the good. Ironically, the harder we try to solidify our memories—even the good ones—the less likely they are to bring us joy.

That makes no sense. Why wouldn't happy memories bring us joy?

Whenever we lock in a memory, we fix in our minds "this is exactly how the event transpired." Then we base our actions on that rendition of the truth. The problem is, it's virtually impossible for any memory to represent the *whole* truth. In clinging to one interpretation, we exclude any other memories that may surface later on. Our world automatically narrows. Say your college roommate comes to visit and, in reminiscing, tells her version of what went on at your senior prom. Do you reject her memories out of hand because they're not in line with your own, or do you welcome this new and broader view?

What if I don't want to remember everything? If I've done something embarrassing, say, or offended a friend, I'd just as soon not be reminded.

Who said, "Happiness is nothing more than good health and a bad memory"? Still, I bet you'd be happier in the long run if you cleared things up with your friend. How honest and forthright we are in the present determines our happiness in the future. We can forget what we don't want to remember, but the body never lies. What we won't face tends to turn up anyway, in nightmares, illness, injuries, anxiety, depression, or fatigue.

If memory can make me ill, can it also make me healthy and happy?
Memory allows us to use our past experience as a guide to our behavior. Theoretically, we learn from our mistakes. There are also ways to work deliberately with memory to increase happiness. One is to keep a happiness journal. During the day, jot down anything that makes you happy or that you're grateful for. Later, when you're feeling low, the journal entries will jog your memory: "Oh, yes, I'm happy when I'm cooking, or when I'm listening to music." In Tennessee Williams' play *The Glass Menagerie*, one of the characters says, "In memory everything seems to happen to music." Which of your memories are triggered by music? If I hear Richard Anthony singing

❝ Recollection is the only paradise from which we cannot be turned out. ❞

JEAN PAUL RICHTER (1763–1825)

"Oui, Va Plus Loin"—"Walk on By" in French—I'm immediately back at the Casablanca, sipping wine with my first great love. Don't, for heaven's sake, play music that reminds you of sad times unless you're itching for a good cry. But by all means put on *Aida* if the Triumphal March reminds you of that Roman holiday when you saw the production at the Baths of Caracalla, live elephants and all.

When I'm stressed, I can't remember anything. I miss appointments. I forget where I put things.

One of the first steps in reclaiming memories is to quiet the chatter in our heads. Meditation helps, or practices like Chi Kung and yoga with breathing techniques to calm and center you. Aerobic exercise sends oxygen-rich blood to the brain. And since memory is also responsive to mental exercise, anything from the daily crossword to learning a new skill will help. People with full, rich lives have that many more opportunities to lay down happy memories. Travel provides novelty and a ready supply of memories.

My sister and I often argue over what happened in our childhood. We have completely different memories of the same events. How can we tell who's right?

As we've seen, absolutes like right and wrong don't apply to memory. Two people experiencing the same event will recall different elements of it. That's what makes eyewitness testimony so confounding. You and your sister filtered childhood events through your thoughts and emotions at the time, so it's only natural that your memories differ. Far more important than the actual events are the emotions they triggered. If something made us happy in the past, it's the happiness we want to recreate, not the event itself.

Let's see if I understand you. If I was really happy on a trip to Paris, I wouldn't have to actually go back there to feel that happiness again?

Your body has a sense-memory of being in Paris. If you can connect with that, you can re-experience the happiness. That's one reason physical souvenirs are so helpful. Maybe you bought a little model of the Eiffel Tower in Paris, and now every time you look at it, it triggers the memory "I love Paris," and you feel good. You don't have to revisit Paris to revisit the happiness you felt there. As a friend of mine pointed out, "Happiness is a feeling, not an accumulation of experiences."

Dialogue **20**

FAVORABLE OPTIONS

How to make wise decisions

Life is one choice after another. For or against. This or that. Too many options and we feel overwhelmed. Too few and we complain. But whatever circumstances we encounter, we can always choose to find satisfaction. Happiness isn't something that just happens to us. It's a decision we make.

*Recently friends visited from abroad and were amazed at the array
of choices they encountered in the shops and restaurants, and in
cultural events and entertainment. "You're lucky to have so many
options," they said. I meanwhile had just spent a frustrating
half-hour in front of a display of phone cards, trying to figure out
which of the forty-odd cards might suit my needs. I finally gave up
and left the store empty-handed. Am I the only one who feels
stymied by so many choices?*

I think a lot of us are overwhelmed. Sociologist Barry
Schwartz calls it "choice overload." Just walking up
and down the aisles of the average gourmet food
shop is enough to make you feel you've eaten a five-
course meal. The ability to choose how we live and
what we buy is a basic freedom we cherish. And I dare
say most of us welcome options—up to a point. But
after that, as with your phone cards, more options just
make a decision harder. One product becomes virtually
indistinguishable from another, so we either fall back
on what's familiar, or give up and make no decision.

*Then why do our friends think we're so lucky? Don't they see how
frustrating too much choice can be?*

Having fewer options sounds like heaven to us—for
one thing, it would reduce the time spent shopping

and free us up for more important matters. But for people who have very little, lack of choice can make life harder. Often they're forced to spend an inordinate amount of time just rounding up the bare necessities. We're confronted with so many decisions on so many levels that it's hard for us to imagine what it would be like to live in an environment over which we had little control.

ONE THING ABOUT LIMITED OPTIONS—THERE ARE FEWER EXPECTATIONS. IF YOU DON'T KNOW SOMETHING EXISTS, YOU WON'T BOTHER LOOKING FOR IT.

In that respect, people with fewer options are probably happier than people who realize they have unlimited options but can't afford to pursue any of them. Longing does not lead to happiness.

That makes me think of what a production shopping is for me.
Most people, if they need something, go into a store, check out the
alternatives, choose one, pay for it, and leave. Case closed. Me?
I run all over town comparing models and prices, and by the time I
get home, I'm exhausted. Half the time I wonder if what I bought
was even worth the effort. Isn't there a less stressful way to choose?

Barry Schwartz calls the kind of people who don't make a big thing of shopping "satisficers." Once they find something "good enough" to meet their standards, that's it. They don't waste time second-guessing. You sound more like Schwartz's "maximizer" —the consummate consumer who spends hours in preparation, then won't stop looking until every possibility is exhausted. Logic says maximizers should be happier than satisficers, who are willing to just settle. But as Schwartz points out in *The Paradox of Choice*, the opposite is true. Maximizers get so caught up in wondering if they missed out on something better that they're unable to enjoy what they have.

Ouch. That's me. What can I do about it?

We all need to rethink our attitudes about choice. We're so conditioned to believe that life involves thousands of choices every day that we feel impelled to make decisions about even the small stuff. Here's where Eastern and Western thinking diverge:

MINDFULNESS PRACTICE WOULD TELL YOU TO SLOW DOWN AND OBSERVE YOUR MIND MOMENT BY MOMENT, AS YOU DECIDE *NOT THIS, NOT THAT, NOT THIS, YES THAT.*

Schwartz takes a more Western view, suggesting that we learn to

"CHOOSE WHEN TO CHOOSE."

We don't have to make decisions about things we do on automatic, like our morning bathing-and-dressing routine. We can also train ourselves to be more like satisficers—okay with "good enough" choices.

" Our life is frittered away by detail ... Simplify, simplify. "

HENRY DAVID THOREAU (1817–62)

I'm not sure I'd be happy if I didn't go all out to make the best choice possible.

But don't you see? Placing such demands on yourself isn't making you happy. So why not *choose* a different way? What's hardest about choice is that by definition it means we can't have it all. Every decision involves leaving something behind. We all know people who try so hard to keep their options open, they end up living by default. Life makes the choices for them. They may not even realize that the reason they're so resentful about what happens to them is that they've abdicated power to choose. The happiest people I know don't wait for circumstances to decide their fate. They're proactive when choice is called for.

But won't we feel better if we leave ourselves some wiggle room— only buy things we can return if we change our minds, for example?

That's the conventional wisdom. But if you're retraining yourself to be a happy decision-maker, you might want to follow Schwartz's advice: "Make your decisions irreversible."

No way! I'd have a closet full of unworn clothes and a miserable marriage.

His logic is: if we know we can return it, we will return it. Closing off that option would mean no more second-guessing but instead putting our energy into reassuring ourselves we've made a good decision. The same thing applies to marriage. Maybe we'd enjoy it more if we didn't have that escape clause in the back of our minds. Mind you, I'm not suggesting we abolish divorce. Just that we start giving major decisions more consideration than whether or not to buy that Armani jacket.

What's this business about choosing happiness? Is it really a matter of choice? Aren't we born with a basic happiness level that goes up and down a little but essentially stays the same?

The idea we have a genetic "set-point" of happiness from which we hardly deviate is no longer considered the whole story. There's pretty convincing evidence that we can retrain our brains and emotions to a far greater degree than was thought. True, some people are just naturally sunny. But for many of us, happiness is a decision. We set an intention to be happy, then follow up with conscious effort, such as reframing negative thinking and becoming more flexible.

So if I'm unhappy one day it means I'm doing something wrong? Changing moods are a reality. Choosing happiness doesn't mean ignoring or overriding negative emotions but acknowledging and transforming them. Happiness is a posture toward life. Viktor Frankl, the psychiatrist who developed logotherapy out of his experience in concentration camps, observed that the one thing the Nazis could not take from the prisoners was "the last of the human freedoms—to choose one's attitude in any given set of circumstances." We hear countless stories of people who are happy despite adversity. Even Abraham Lincoln—known for his black depressions—said,

" Most people are just about as happy as they make up their minds to be."

Further Reading

ACKERMAN, DIANE
An Alchemy of Mind
Scribner, 2004

BECK, MARTHA
The Joy Diet
Crown, 2003

BURNS, DAVID D., MD
Feeling Good
Quill, 2000

CHÖDRÖN, PEMA
The Places That Scare You
Shambhala, 2001

CHOPRA, DEEPAK, MD
The Book of Secrets
Harmony, 2004

CSIKSZENTMIHALYI, MIHALY
Flow
Harper & Row, 1990

CUSHNIR, HOWARD RAPHAEL
Unconditional Bliss
Quest, 2000

DAS, LAMA SURYA
*Letting Go of the Person You
    Used to Be*
Broadway, 2003

EKMAN, PAUL
Emotions Revealed
Henry Holt, 2003

EPICTETUS
The Art of Living
*A new interpretation by Sharon
    Lebell*
Harper San Francisco, 1995

FOSTER, RICK AND GREG HICKS
How We Choose to Be Happy
G.P. Putnam's Sons, 1999
Perigee, 2000

HOUSDEN, ROGER
Ten Poems to Change Your Life
Harmony, 2001

HIS HOLINESS THE DALAI LAMA
    AND HOWARD C. CUTLER, MD
The Art of Happiness
Riverhead Books, 1998

JAMISON, KAY REDFIELD
Exuberance
Alfred A. Knopf, 2004

LERNER, HARRIET
Fear and Other Uninvited Guests
Harper Collins, 2004

MACDONALD, LUCY
Learn to Be an Optimist
Duncan Baird/Chronicle Books,
    2004

MARAR, ZIYAD
The Happiness Paradox
Reaktion Books, 2003

NEEDLEMAN, JACOB
Money and the Meaning of Life
Doubleday Currency, 1991

O'DONOHUE, JOHN
Beauty: The Invisible Embrace
Harper Collins, 2004

REMEM, RACHEL NAOMI, MD
My Grandfather's Blessings
Riverhead, 2000

RICARD, MATTHIEU
*Plaidoyer pour le Bonheur
(Plea for Happiness)*
NiL editions, 2003

RUSSELL, BERTRAND
The Conquest of Happiness
Liveright, 1996

RYAN, M.J.
The Power of Patience
Broadway, 2003

SALZBERG, SHARON
A Heart as Wide as the World
Shambhala, 1997

SELIGMAN, MARTIN E.P., PHD
Authentic Happiness
The Free Press, 2002

THARP, TWYLA
The Creative Habit
Simon & Schuster, 2003

Acknowledgments

INTRODUCTION
p.6 "the happiness business"
Lester Lanin obituary, *The New York Times*, October 29, 2004
p.7 the "Duchenne smile" Paul Ekman, *Emotions Revealed*, Owl, 2004, pp.204–6
p.10 "upward spiral"
L. Frederickson, "The Value of Positive Emotions," *American Scientist*, Vol. 91, July–August 2003, p.335
p.13 "People have the idea ... "
Alex Barrantes-Tancredi quoted in *The New York Times*, Education Life, August 1, 2004, p.17.

DIALOGUE 1: EMOTIONS
p.17 Paul Ekman, *Emotions Revealed*, Owl, 2004, p.44
p.19 "Really attend to them ... "
Destructive Emotions, a scientific dialogue with the Dalai Lama, narrated by Daniel Goleman, Bantam, 2003, p.291
p.20 "People who ... " Barbara L. Frederickson, "The Value of Positive Emotions," *American Scientist*, Vol. 91, July–August 2003, p.335

DIALOGUE 2: KINDNESS
p.26 I read about a young boy ...
Lisa Belkin, "The Lessons of Classroom 506," *The New York Times Magazine*, Sunday, September 12, 2004.
p.27 "In one way or another I believe we are called ... " Lorna Kelly, *The Camel Knows the Way*, second ed., 2004, published by Lorna Kelly, P.O. Box 1788, Radio City Station, New York, NY 10101-1788
The Dalai Lama points out ... His Holiness the Dalai Lama and Howard C. Cutler, MD, *The Art of Happiness*, Riverhead, 1998, p.114.
p.28 Sharon Salzberg, *A Heart as Wide as the World*, Shambhala, 1997, p.77.
"Be a good person ... " His Holiness the Dalai Lama and Howard C. Cutler, MD, *The Art of Happiness at Work*, Riverhead, 2003, p.37
p.29 being kind ... *The Art of Happiness*, p.179

DIALOGUE 3: UNCERTAINTY
p.34 Alan Watts, *The Wisdom of Insecurity*, Vintage, 1951, pp.59–60
p.36 Pema Chödrön, *The Places That Scare You*, Shambhala, 2001, p.7

DIALOGUE 4: CREATIVITY
p.40 "Creativity is a habit ... "
Twyla Tharp, *The Creativity Habit*, Simon & Schuster, 2003, p.5
follow roughly the same path
Mihaly Csikszentmihalyi, *Creativity*, HarperPerennial, 1996, pp.79–80.
p.41–43 first step ... Compare the stages of creativity identified by Henri Poincaré, summarized by V. N. Narayan in "Creativity is Your Birthright," www.lifepositive.com/Mind/arts/creativity/geniuses.asp
p.43 creativity as "connecting to the Divine ... " Matthew Fox, *Creativity*, Tarcher/Putnam, 2002, p.5
p.44 "Creativity causes the soul to rejoice," the mystic Meister Eckhart ... quoted by Matthew Fox in *Creativity*, p.68.
p.44–45 Julia Cameron, *The Artist's Way*, Tarcher/Putnam, 1992; *Walking in This World*, Tarcher/Putnam, 2002. Author's conversations with J. Cameron
p.45 "Cultivate curiosity and interest ... " Mihaly Csikszentmihalyi, *Creativity: Flow and the Psychology of Discovery and Invention*, HarperPerennial, 1996, p.347
Creativity background, general:
John Daido Loori, *The Zen of Creativity*, Ballantine, 2003

DIALOGUE 5: PURPOSE
p.49 "Midway along the journey ... " Dante Alighieri, "The Divine Comedy," *The Portable Dante*, trans. Mark Musa, Penguin, 1995, p.3.
p.50 "The breeze at dawn ... "
Jelaluddin Rumi, *The Essential Rumi*, trans. Coleman Barks with John Moyne, Castle Books, 1995, p.36.
p.51 "Consistent purpose is not enough ... " Bertrand Russell, *The Conquest of Happiness*, Liveright, 1996, p.169
p.55 "*Live* the questions" Rainer Maria Rilke, *Letters to a Young Poet*, trans. M.D. Herter Norton, W.W. Norton, 1954, p.35.

DIALOGUE 6: OTHER PEOPLE
p.56 "Only connect!" E.M. Forster, *Howards End*, Vintage, 1921, p.186.

DIALOGUE 7: TIME

p.67 "Hope is the cordial ... "
Samuel Richardson, *Clarissa*, Vol.3,
AMS, 1990, p.266.

p.68 "the thing with feathers ... "
Emily Dickinson, *The Oxford Book of
American Verse,* F.O. Mathiessen, ed.,
Oxford, 1950, p.419.

**p.69 "Real generosity toward the
future lies in giving all to the
present"** Albert Camus, "Beyond
Nihilism," *The Rebel,* 1954.

DIALOGUE 8: ACCEPTANCE

**p.72 "Muddy water, let stand,
becomes clear"** Lao Tse, *Tao Te
Ching,* Ch.15.

**p.74 "Fatalism is the lazy man's
way ... "** Natalie Clifford Barney,
quoted in George Wickes, *The
Amazon of Letters,* Putnam, 1976,
Ch.10.

**p.75 introduces us to Herman
Wallace** *A Revolution in Kindness,*
Anita Roddick Books, 2003,
pp.132–134.

DIALOGUE 10: WEALTH

**p.85 Oprah Winfrey gave a new
Pontiac** Keith Naughton, "A Car Is
Born," *Newsweek,* Sept. 27, 2004,
p.40.

p.86 Sociologist Tim Kasser found
The High Price of Materialism, MIT
Press, 2002, p.11

**p.87 contentment the greatest
form of wealth** Lama Surya Das,
"The Wisdom of Letting Go," *Ask
the Lama,* www.beliefnet.com.

"the only true wealth" Jacob
Needleman, *Money and the Meaning
of Life,* Doubleday Currency, 1991,
p.212.

p.89 people with volunteer jobs
Ziyad Marar, *The Happiness Paradox,*
Reaktion, 2003, p.135.

p. 90 "the good life ... " Leaf Van
Boven and Thomas D. Gilovich, "To
Do or to Have? That Is the
Question," *Journal of Personality and
Social Psychology,* December 2003,
pp.1193–1202.

**p.90–91 "whatever is sufficient
... "** Toinette Lippe, *Nothing Left
Over,* Tarcher/Penguin, 2002, p.37

**p.91 "When you stop chasing
more ... "** Lynn Twist, "A Life of
Abundance," *Spirituality & Health,*
April 2004, p.31

**calculus for determining your real
income** Joe Dominguez and Vicki
Robin, *Your Money or Your Life,*
Penguin, 1999, pp. 59–68.

DIALOGUE 11: BEAUTY

p.92 "only form of the spiritual"
Thomas Mann, *Death in Venice and
Other Tales,* Penguin, 1998, p.334.

**p.94 "Beautiful people aren't
perfect"** Zeta Graff, interview by
Olivia Falcon, "Tales from the Powder
Room," *Tatler,* September 2004.

**Think of the actor Denzel
Washington** Geoffrey Cowley, "The
Biology of Beauty," *Newsweek,* June
3, 1996, p.62.

**p.95 The poet A.E. Housman
contended** J.O. Urmson, "What
Makes a Situation Aesthetic?" in
Philosophy Looks at the Arts, Joseph
Margolis, ed., Scribner, 1962, p.21.

**p.97 "If eyes were made for
seeing"** Ralph Waldo Emerson,
"The Rhodora," *The Oxford Book of
American Verse,* F. O. Matthiesen,
ed., Oxford Univ. Press, 1950, p.67.

"Beauty is truth, truth beauty"
John Keats, "Ode on a Grecian Urn,"
The Oxford Book of English Verse, Sir
Arthur Quiller-Couch, ed., Oxford
Univ. Press, 1939, p.746.

p.98 "trifling amusements" The

Nicomachean Ethics in Aristotle,
trans. Philip Wheelwright, Odyssey,
1951, p.264.

"nobly beautiful" *The
Nichomachean Ethics,* p.186

**p.99 "The graced eye can glimpse
beauty"** John O'Donohue, *Beauty:
The Invisible Embrace,* HarperCollins,
2004, p.19.

p.101 "Think of all the beauty ... "
Anne Frank, *Diary of a Young Girl,*
Doubleday, 1991, p.210.

DIALOGUE 12: LOVE

p.104 All are stages of love Helen
Fisher, *Why We Love: The Nature and
Chemistry of Romantic Love,* Henry
Holt, 2004.

p.107 "Oh, my Beloved!" Jalalludin
Rumi in *The Inner Treasure: An
Introduction to the World's Sacred
and Mystical Writing,* trans. Jonathan
Star, Tarcher/Putnam, 1999, p.111.

DIALOGUE 13: LAUGHTER

p.111 Children laugh "Science of
Laughter,"
www.discoveryhealth.co.uk.

"laughter ambassador training"
Dr. Ronald Schutzbach,
www.hahahahaha.org.

**p. 112 we don't laugh because
we're happy** William James, "The
Gospel of Relaxation," *Selected
Papers on Philosophy,* Dent/Dutton,
1918.

"a calisthenic for body and soul"
Robert R. Provine, *Laughter: A
Scientific Investigation,* Viking, 2000,
p.190.

"real religion is ... " Alan Watts, *In
My Own Way: An Autobiography,*
Vintage, 1973, p.69.

**p.113 relaxes our muscles ...
stimulates the immune system**
Lee Berk, DrPh, et al, *American*

Journal of Medical Science, 1989, vol. 298, pp. 390–396; Alternative Therapies, March 2001, pp.62–76; William F. Fry, Jr., Journal of the American Medical Association, 1992, vol. 267, no. 13, pp. 1857–1858; Kathleen Doheny, "Lighten Up," http://webmd.com.
"laughing yoga" Dr. Madan Kataria, www.laughteryoga.org
p.114 toning 15 facial muscles "Science of Laughter," www.discoveryhealth.co.uk.
p.115 "Ten minutes of ... laughter" Norman Cousins, Anatomy of an Illness as Perceived by the Patient, Norton, 1979, p.39
20 minutes a day Pragito Dove, "Let's Get Serious About Laughter!," www.newconnexion.net.
p.116 20 percent of ... laughter "Science of Laughter," www.discoveryhealth.co.uk.
"the shortest distance ... " Victor Borge obituary, Reuters, Dec. 23, 2000.

DIALOGUE 14: SUCCESS
p.123 identify the biggest success of their lives "Your Words," Real Simple, September 2004, p.55.
p.123–124 "... if your children aren't successful" Ted Turner interview, "Charlie Rose," PBS-TV, July 23, 2004.
p.124 "to know even one life ... " Bessie A. Stanley, "Success," Modern Woman, 1905, www.chebucto.ns.ca/Philosophy/Sui-Generis/Emerson/success.htm.
"Success makes life easier" Bruce Springsteen, interview, August 1992.
p.125 "Be satisfied with success" Marcus Aurelius, Meditations, Book IX, 29.

DIALOGUE 15: FAITH
p.127 "Belief is the insistence that the truth ..." Alan W. Watts, The Wisdom of Insecurity, Vintage, 1951, p.24.
"primal anthropological act" Gerard Hall, "Multi-faith Dialogue in Conversation with Raimon Panikkar," Australian Association for the Study of Religions Annual Conference, July 2003.
p.128 "our beliefs" Fenton Johnson interview with Dan Mitchell, "Speaking of Faith" web editor, Minnesota Public Radio, 2003.
"refers to a man's ultimate trust" Ian Barbour quoted in Robert E. Emmons, The Psychology of Ultimate Concerns, Guilford Press, 1999, p.96.
p. 129 Sharon Salzberg, Faith, Riverhead, 2002.
p.132 "At this point, good business" Mihaly Csikszentmihalyi, Good Business, Viking, 2003, p.210.
p.132–133 "the ongoing weaving ... " Sharon Parks quoted in The Psychology of Ultimate Concerns, Guilford Press, 1999, p.114
p.133 "Everything we make .ı. " Sara Davidson, "What They Did for Bliss," O:The Oprah Magazine, March 2004, p.243.

DIALOGUE 16: SERENITY
p.134 "the still point of the turning world" T.S. Eliot, "Burnt Norton," Four Quartets, Harcourt, Brace, 1943, p.5.

DIALOGUE 18: NATURE
p.150 "Glory be to God for dappled things" Gerald Manley Hopkins, "Pied Beauty," The New Oxford Book of English Verse, Sir Arthur Quiller-Couch, ed., Oxford, 1939, p.1011.

p.152 "this quality of Lilith's" Barbara Black Koltuv, The Book of Lilith, Nicolas-Hays, 1986, p.25.
p.155 no more blessed existence Roger Scruton , Animal Rights and Wrongs, Metro, London, 2000, p.100
"Tao gives all things life" Tao Te Ching, Ch.51, in The Inner Treasure, trans. by Jonathan Star, Tarcher/Putnam, 1999, p.35.

DIALOGUE 19: MEMORY
p.158 "the diary that we all carry" Oscar Wilde, The Importance of Being Earnest, Act II.
"nothing but a collective hunch" Jane Wagner, The Search for Signs of Intelligent Life in the Universe, performed by Lily Tomlin.
p.159 "the most faithful autobiography ... " Fawn M. Brodie, No Man Knows My History, Knopf, 1946, p.275.
p.161 "everything seems to happen to music" Tennessee Williams, The Glass Menagerie, Scene 1.
Appreciation to Sandra Weinberg, CSW, for substantial contributions to the Memory dialogue.

DIALOGUE 20: CHOICE
p.165 Sociologist Barry Schwartz calls it B. Schwartz, The Paradox of Choice, HarperCollins, 2004.
p.171 "last of the human freedoms" Viktor E. Frankl, Man's Search for Meaning, Pocket, 1963, p.104.

Index

A
Anthony, Richard 161
Aristotle 98
St. Augustine 127

B
Barbour, Ian 128
Barney, Natalie Clifford 75
Beard, Peter 46
Borge, Victor 116
Brodie, Fawn 159
Buddha, the 35, 120, 129
Bush, President George W. 87

C
Cameron, Julia 45
Camus, Albert 69
Carlyle, Thomas 89
Chödrön, Pema 36
Confucius 122
Cousins, Norman 114–115
Csikszentimihalyi, Mihaly 44, 45, 132

D
Dalai Lama 6, 19, 27, 28–29
Dante 49
Davidson, Sarah 133
Diana, Princess of Wales 123
Dickens, Charles
   Great Expectations 66
   A Christmas Carol 24, 26
Dickinson, Emily 68
Dominguez, Joe and Robin, Vicki 91
Dukkha 120

E
Eckhart, Meister 44
Edison, Thomas 43
Einstein, Albert 53
Ekman, Paul 17
Eliot, T.S. 134
Emerson, Ralph Waldo 96, 97
Epictetus 71
Erasmus 51

F
Fischer, Bobby 33
Fisher, Helen 104
Forster, E.M. 56
Fox, Matthew 43
Frank, Anne 101
Frankl, Viktor 171
Fredrickson, Barbara 20–21
Freud, Sigmund 8

G
Goleman, Daniel 19
St. Gregory of Sinai 133

H
Hawking, Stephen 68
Hopkins, Gerald Manley 150
Housman, A.E. 95

J
Jainism 79
James, William 112
Jefferson, Thomas 78
Johnson, Fenton 128

K
Kasser, Tim 86
Keats, John 97

Keller, Helen 68
Kelly, Lorna 27
Koltuv, Barbara Black 152
Kornfield, Jack 55

L
Lamb, Charles 24
Lincoln, Abraham 171
Lippe, Toinette 90
Lowell, James Russell 42

M
Mann, Thomas 92
Marar, Ziyad 89
Marcus Aurelius 18, 125

N
Nagarjuna 87
Needleman, Jacob 87

O
O'Donohue, John 98, 99
Onassis, Jacqueline Kennedy 123

P
Pannikar, Raimon 127
Parker, Dorothy 117
Parks, Sharon 132–133
Pascal, Blaise 101
Piaf, Edith 157
Plato 12, 79
Provine, Robert 112

R
Reeve, Christopher 68
Richardson, Samuel 67
Richter, Jean Paul 161
Rilke, Rainer Maria 34
Roddick, Anita 75
Roth, Gabrielle 136

Rowling, J.K. 46
Rumi 50, 62, 107
Russell, Bertrand 51

S
Salzberg, Sharon 28, 129, 130
Schwartz, Barry 165, 167, 168
Scruton, Roger 155
September 11, 2001 37, 87, 159
Socrates 12
Springsteen, Bruce 124
Stanley, Bessie A. 123–124

T
Tao Te Ching 72, 155
Teresa, Mother 26, 52, 53, 98
Tharp, Twyla 40, 44
Thoreau, Henry David 169
Tomlin, Lily 158
Turner, Ted 123
Twist, Lynn 91

V
Van Boven, Leaf and Tomas Gilovich 89

W
Wallace, Herman 75
Washington, Denzel 94
Watts, Alan 35, 113, 127
Wilde, Oscar 158
Williams, Tennessee 161
Winfrey, Oprah 85, 133